THE FIRST AMENDMENT—THE CHALLENGE OF NEW TECHNOLOGY

THE FIRST AMENDMENT—THE CHALLENGE OF NEW TECHNOLOGY

Edited by
SIG MICKELSON
with
ELENA MIER Y TERAN

PRAEGER

New York
Westport, Connecticut
London

Library of Congress Cataloging-in-Publication Data

The First amendment—the challenge of new technology / [edited by] Sig Mickelson with Elena Mier y Teran.

    p.   cm.

    Papers presented at a conference convened in November 1987 by the San Diego Communications Council.

    Includes index.

    ISBN 0-275-93088-2 (alk. paper)

    1. Freedom of information—United States—Congresses. 2. Freedom of the press—United States—Congresses. 3. Telecommunication—Law and legislation—United States—Congresses. I. Mickelson, Sig. II. Mier y Teran, Elena. III. San Diego Communications Council.

KF4774.A75F573 1989

342.73'0853—dc19

[347.302853]   88-19037

Copyright © 1989 by Sig Mickelson

All rights reserved. No portion of this book may be reproduced, by any process or technique, without the express written consent of the publisher.

Library of Congress Catalog Card Number: 88-19037
ISBN: 0-275-93088-2

First published in 1989

Praeger Publishers, One Madison Avenue, New York, NY 10010
A division of Greenwood Press, Inc.

Printed in the United States of America

The paper used in this book complies with the Permanent Paper Standard issued by the National Information Standards Organization (Z39.48—1984).

10 9 8 7 6 5 4 3 2 1

Contents

	Preface	vii
	Introduction	ix
1.	TECHNOLOGY AND HUMAN FREEDOM *J. Richard Munro*	1
2.	THE FIRST AMENDMENT—ITS CURRENT CONDITION *Craig R. Smith, Henry Geller, Patrick D. Maines, and Daniel L. Brenner*	9
3.	THE FIRST AMENDMENT—FORCES OF CHANGE *Richard M. Schmidt, Jr., John Redpath, Jr., Lee Burdick, Edward T. Reilly, Jr., and Henry Geller*	33
4.	RESPONSIBILITIES AND RIGHTS OF THE MEDIA *David Laventhol*	55
5.	THE FIRST AMENDMENT—NATIONAL SECURITY *J. Laurent Scharff and Jack E. Thomas*	63

6. THE FIRST AMENDMENT—RIGHTS OF
   PRIVACY 79
   *Edwin H. James, Elliot E. Maxwell, Tony Acone,
   and Fred W. Weingarten*

7. REMARKS 101
   James H. Quello and Al Swift

   Chronology of First Amendment Issues 107

   Index 113

   About the Editors and Contributors 117

Preface

The suggestion that San Diego host a conference designed to examine the capability of the First Amendment to cope with communications technology in the amendment's third century was first broached at a meeting of the executive committee of the San Diego Communications Council in early 1987. The council is an organization of businesses and individuals in the San Diego area concerned with the future of communications. It has strong support, both moral and administrative, from the College of Professional Studies and Fine Arts at San Diego State University.

The council has been principally concerned since its inception in mid 1986 with two aspects of communications technology:

1. What will happen to existing barriers separating different branches of the communications industry as new technologies based largely on electronics permit encroachment across traditional lines of demarcation?
2. How will regulators respond to new methods of communicating using new devices that were not foreseen when regulations were written? And what of the First Amendment to the Constitution? Will the amendment continue to be flexible enough to adapt to new communications technologies? Will the protections afforded historically to the print media be extended to new processes for communicating? Or, conversely, if the print media begin to use new electronic devices will they lose their First Amendment protections?

The two hundredth anniversary of the ratification of the United States Constitution, celebrated in 1987, supplied the rationale for emphasizing the constitutional aspects of the developing dilemma. It is evident that the introduction of new technologies will subject the First Amendment to stresses exceeding anything in its past history. How it adapts to accelerating change will inevitably have a profound impact on the degree of freedom to be exercised by all manner of communications media in the future.

The unanimous decision of the council was to proceed, using the title "The First Amendment—Third Century." In keeping with the Communications Council's theme it was decided to stress the possible impact of the adoption of new communications technologies with respect to the tensions they may impose on the First Amendment. It was determined that participants should represent a broad mix of talents and experiences: practitioners in newspapers, magazines, broadcasting and cable; regulators and former regulators; communications theorists and educators and, if possible, one or more members of the United States Congress with particular interest in communications.

Special commendation for their efforts in organizing the event and in assuring its success is owed to Terry Churchill, San Diego area vice president for Pacific Bell and chairman of the San Diego Communications Council; Ann Burr, president of Southwestern Cable and conference finance chairman; Merrill J. Lessley, dean of the School of Professional Studies and Fine Arts at San Diego State University; and to John Witherspoon, director of the Communications Center at San Diego State, and Herman Land, Van Deerlin professor of telecommunications and film at San Diego State, who co-chaired the program committee.

Introduction

For most readers the language of the First Amendment to the Constitution of the United States as it applies to media freedom is deceptively simple: "Congress shall make no law . . . abridging the freedom of speech, or of the press. . . . " It was drafted in an era when the printing press was the sole mechanical device available for mass communication and the human voice could reach only as far as its sound could penetrate. The few newspapers that were published were single-sheet journals of opinion with minuscule circulations, a few hundred at the most. A few books, some early magazines, and irregularly printed hortatory pamphlets constituted the full roster of the communications media of the era. But even in that uncomplicated environment application of the First Amendment was not easy. It was always difficult to define *abridge* and it has never been fully decided what constitutes *freedom*.

If it was difficult to define *freedom* and *abridgement* then difficulties have grown exponentially since the First Amendment's ratification in 1791, some 200 years ago. As we near the end of the twentieth century we live in an age of what can only be described as communications miracles. New discoveries, new devices, new processes, and new technologies for sorting, storing, and retrieving information and transmitting it at the speed of light are pouring out of laboratories and factories at a breathtaking rate. The First Amendment that has served so well for so long must now adapt to the introduction of new technologies that even the fertile mind of Benjamin Franklin could never have dreamed of.

The amendment was able to accommodate, although not without controversy, the introduction of the telegraph, the telephone, the transoceanic cable, radio, television, cable television, the computer and the communications satellite, all the while maintaining the basic freedoms that it was designed to protect.

We know now, however, that the past is only prologue to astonishing new technological advances that are continuing to revolutionize the processes by which we store, retrieve, and communicate information. Technological advances are tumbling on top of one another so fast that there is little time to sit down, catch one's breath, and plan for the future.

In this era of turbulent change what role will the First Amendment play? Will it continue to protect the citizen's rights, and preserve democratic freedoms? Or will it be trampled under in the rush to the new high-tech information age? Does it have the flexibility to keep up with the pace of technology? More specifically, will it be able to sort out the proper roles for competing industries as technology makes it possible for one to encroach on what have been sacrosanct areas reserved exclusively for another?

It was to seek answers to those and related questions that the San Diego Communications Council convened a conference in November 1987 to which it gave the title "The First Amendment—Third Century." The conference was described as "an examination of the First Amendment's ability to cope with an era of dramatic change."

The two-year-old San Diego Communications Council was founded to explore as thoroughly as its available resources would permit the communications world of the future. The varied assortment of communicators, manufacturers, educators, communications users, and research specialists in the council had been brought together by a common curiosity as to where communications technology is leading us. At what point, they wanted to know, will previously well-defined barriers between discrete businesses break down as new technological devices encourage expansion across the old lines of demarcation? How will the regulators respond as new devices and new processes come onto the market place? How will the First Amendment cope with complexities that would have been regarded as irresponsible dreams as recently as a generation ago? Is the First Amendment, in fact, flexible enough to cope with the miracles of modern communications technology?

We know now that the technologies available for mass communication are speeding from the fertile minds of scientists onto drawing boards and into production at a pace that we could never have anticipated as recently as a decade ago. The direction in which they will take us, however, remains obscure.

- What new miracles will fiber optics perform?
- What about new, faster, and more powerful micro chips?
- How much impact will the harnessing of laser beams have on the processes of communicating?
- Will electronic printing and distribution replace the conventional printing press that depends on carrier or mail delivery?
- Will the telephone company's traditional twisted pair of copper wires give way to faster, higher capacity, more versatile successors, including fiber? Or to some form of wireless electronic communication?
- What new wonders can we expect from satellites?
- What will happen to traditional businesses as change continues and accelerates?

The First Amendment has survived its first 200 years in remarkably good health. Whatever may be its weaknesses it has been a powerful force in creating a tradition of freedom of speech, press, and thought that is unmatched anywhere in the world. It is still not certain, however, whether broadcasting is entitled to the same freedom of expression that pertains to the printed media. The relationship of the First Amendment to cable has still not been fully sorted out.

What now happens to newspapers if they begin to distribute their product electronically? Will they continue to elicit the full support of the First Amendment? Or will their electronic output be subjected to some form of licensing comparable to that enforced on the broadcast media?

And what about cable? If telephone companies are able to deliver a vast array of services and entertainment into the home by means of fiber optics, will cable be able to retain its monopoly as a broadband communications service?

And what is the future of telephone companies if cable replaces its coaxial cables with fiber and is able to deliver an addressable person-to-person communications service?

And what happens to the right of privacy as a constantly growing volume of private information about the individual finds its way into computer memories and is available for easy access by a growing number of agencies, institutions and even individuals through a broad array of communications services?

An equally fascinating question relates to the relationship between the First Amendment and the increasing remote-sensing capabilities of satellites. If images from satellites relayed to news media are regarded by government officials as being dangerous to the interests of the United States, does the government or a governmental agency have the right under the Constitution to impose censorship? Or does the right of free press under the First Amendment prevail?

Arriving at reasonable answers is critically important. That in essence is the reason for convening the conference. Nothing, it is obvious, can be solved by a day of talk, no matter how eloquent or thoughtful, but problems can be identified and good minds can be set to thinking about possible solutions. The San Diego Communications Council hopes that the discussion that follows will at the very least call attention to issues involving the First Amendment that need early attention or even better that it will start to create a climate in which emerging controversies can be brought out into the open. The pace of technological invention is now so swift that time is short.

THE FIRST AMENDMENT—THE CHALLENGE OF NEW TECHNOLOGY

1

Technology and Human Freedom

J. Richard Munro

When my old friend and colleague Sig Mickelson invited me to San Diego to participate in this conference on the First Amendment and The Future of Technology, I was initially delighted and flattered. Unfortunately, however, the lure to a trip to San Diego came with a hook, and you're looking at it: I've been asked to give the opening address. The scope of what Sig asked me to speak about was a bit daunting. His letter said that I should discuss, and I quote, "How Time Inc. views the future of government-media relationships with particular reference to the introduction of new technologies and the developments of innovative methods of communicating."

The tussles between government and the media often directly involve Time Inc. But we have a policy that we refer to as "church and state." It means that those of us on the business side don't interfere with the editorial church. Our journalists are free to call things as they see them without worrying at all about the chairman's feelings or his politics. As for speaking about "innovative methods of communicating," I do have a very real and very pragmatic interest in the future effects of new technologies, but I would be less than truthful if I claimed I spent my days studying their feasibility.

I say all of this by way of introduction, because instead of pretending to have a technical or academic expertise I don't possess, I want to speak from my own background as communications executive. But equally, I want to speak as a private citizen who believes that he has a deep and abiding stake in seeing the broadest possible freedom under the First Amendment. That said, I'd like to do at least two things. First, I would like to look at the relationship between freedom of information and technology; second, I will consider whether an amendment written two centuries before TV or cable or media conglomerates still has any real relevance to our future.

Right from the beginning, of course, technology and human freedom are linked. It was technology that created a future in which the idea of free access to information was possible. The technology in question was the printing press. It gave Western society its first taste of mass production, and in the process, it shook the foundations of the existing political and social order. The new availability of books and pamphlets gave access to political theories and scientific views that questioned and ultimately challenged all the old orthodoxies.

As was to happen time and time again, a technological breakthrough created a new audience that the authorities were ultimately unable to control. The system of royal licenses and state controls, of book burnings and even executions, failed to stop the revolution that the printed book set in motion. For a very long time, I think, Western society took for granted this relationship between technological progress and human freedom. The printing press was almost a quasi-religious symbol of our culture's hopes for the future. But gradually we lost faith. With the rise of totalitarian regimes skilled in the use of new technologies such as radio and movies, we came to see technology as the enemy of freedom.

In the brave new world of 1984, television and computers and tape recorders would, it was said, make an all-seeing, all-controlling police state more and more inevitable. But consider what's happening. VCRs and cassettes and the new technologies are subverting efforts to restrict what people watch. As computers revolutionize access to information, as they make entire libraries of facts and opinions available to individuals, they can transform a home or an office into a printing plant. At the flick of a switch, articles and books and essays and statistics and poems can be called up and printed and even distributed electronically.

In the age of our new international economy, when the efficient production and marketing of products depends on the ability to understand computers and their uses, the need for a new and higher literacy is growing dramatically.

Those societies that restrict or deny their people's access to this information find themselves very hard-pressed to compete. Ignorance may be bliss, but as we begin the third century of the Constitution, ignorance is lousy economics, and this puts the traditional proponents of thought control in a real dilemma. How do they modernize and compete in world markets unless they train growing numbers of people to use computers and word processors and video equipment? But once that technology becomes widespread, how do they contain or control the ability to store, call up, even to print ideas or opinions that don't fit into the party line?

Last spring there was a story in the papers about a British journalist in Prague who put this question to a very high Czech official: How, he asked, can the Czech government, which has crusaded against the spread of new technologies and clamped down on free expression, hope to generate sufficient imagination or expertise to compete with the West? In the city of Kafka's birth, the official gave an answer that Kafka would have appreciated, if not approved. In socialist countries, he said, such contradictions do not exist.

Not everyone in the socialist world is so sure. Mikhail Gorbachev is a good example. Without overestimating the significance of *glastnost*, it is safe to say that it is in part an attempt to use to the Soviet's advantage a development the government is increasingly powerless to stop. And in the People's Republic of China, Deng Xiaoping, I believe, faces a similar problem. He set out to create a well-educated class that can master the newest technology. Now that class is demanding new freedoms and equating its freedom with the PRC's future. The government has cracked down, but the problem remains: What to do with the technology and the obvious economic need for it that makes such dissent possible? You can't send microchips to labor camps.

I don't want to make this situation seem any rosier than it is. The instinct for repression is still very strong. In far too many places it is state policy. But the nightmare of a world shackled by an omnipresent Big Brother has not come to pass. Instead, technology is universalizing the scope of the First Amendment.

We Americans, I believe, can take great pride in having conceived and created the ideal that so much of the world aspires to. Yet we, too, have some problems. One of the foremost is the temptation of the government to set itself up as an arbiter of what the American people should and should not know. This temptation did not begin with the Reagan Administration. But this administration certainly has shown a special zeal for giving in to it. From the exclusion of the press from the Grenada invasion, to the secret wars of the CIA; to the disinformation campaign surrounding the raid on Libya, to the whole, sad, sordid mess of Irangate, in which even the president was supposedly kept in the dark, we've seen a growing passion for secrecy and manipulation. Increasingly, we've been told what the government wants us to be told, all in the name of national security.

Let me be careful here. As bad as this administration has been, as obsessed as it has been with barring the media from just about everything except carefully staged photo opportunities, I'm not claiming we're about to become a police state. Our access to different ideas and opinions is breathtaking. The growth of cable and video cassettes, the growing number of magazines and specialty publications, the tremendous volume of book sales, all point to a communications industry as healthy and as vital as at any time in our history. Yet, the threat is there. In a world of incessant international tensions, where the possibility of war or military action is constant and immediate, the prying of the press is frequently depicted as harming our future. Worse, there often seems to be an underlying attitude that the media are disloyal, that their coverage is aimed against the best interests of this country, that they don't give a damn about either truth or the national security.

For my own part, I don't believe these accusations carry a lot of weight. I have been around enough journalists and editors to understand the agony they go through in their attempts to be as objective as they possibly can. And as a Marine in Korea, I never had any reason to resent the reporters who followed us into combat, who risked their lives every day to describe the real war to the people back home.

Yet under the system of laws that we've created for ourselves, my personal opinions of the media, or yours, or for that matter, the president's, aren't really of consequence. In the United States, what matters is the Constitution. What matters is the protection given to the media by the geniuses who designed and drafted our basic body of law, in particular, the First Amendment. We've all heard that amendment so many times it's a little like listening to the Pledge of Allegiance. We're so comfortable with the words we really don't think much about what they mean. But since we're here to talk about its future, maybe the best thing we can do is listen to it just one more time:

Congress shall make no law respecting an establishment of religion, or prohibiting the free exercise thereof, or abridging the freedom of speech or of the press; or the right of the people peaceably to assemble and to petition the government for a redress of grievances.

Short, sweet, and simple. And yet, notice the seemingly odd mix of interests that occurs in this First Amendment: religion and the press joined together in the same breath. I'm sure Tammy Faye and Jim Bakker resent that association, and, for their part, I'm sure a lot of journalists feel the same way.

Two very fundamental freedoms are involved here, of course, but why join them together? The other nine amendments in what we call the Bill of Rights are all devoted to individual concerns—to bail, to trial by jury, to security of property. Why, then, put separation of church and state together with freedom of the press? Weren't these important enough to each be enshrined in a separate article? Or were the framers saying something profoundly basic about the society they were trying to bring into being, about the future of the freedoms they were seeking to secure? Think about it for just a moment. In a phrase that's become increasingly popular, think about "the original intent" of those who framed the First Amendment.

These men didn't have the luxury of presuming upon their freedom the way all of us in this room do. To one degree or another, every king or parliament then in existence asserted its right to decide what was best for the people to believe, what was safe for them to know.

That was the world that our Founders knew, and that was the world they were trying to change. And in order to create a government that rested on the consent of the governed, they set out to protect that consent to make sure it was truly free and truly informed. To do that, they drew very clear and definite lines around the prerogatives of government: first around its ability to take an interest in what people believe, prohibiting government from policing our minds and souls through the operation of an established church; then, in the very same article, ensuring free and unfettered channels of communication and information and expression. They didn't hedge or equivocate. They didn't say that in certain cases or in the face of a particular set of circumstances the press should be curtailed or censored. And this wasn't because they lived in an era where the press, what we now call the media, was a model of civility and unquestioned veracity.

In the eighteenth century, the idea of journalistic objectivity was like the western frontier: unexplored and undeveloped. The newspapers that Madison and Washington read were often slanderous, sometimes scurrilous, always partisan. Some of you may know the old story that when the constitutional convention was held in Philadelphia the town was swamped by a wave of prostitutes and journalists. The former offered the latter cut rates for their services. They said they were extending a courtesy to a kindred profession.

But whatever the personal motivation—or even the personal morality—of the press was in those days, it was not of concern to those who founded our government. They were not interested in the virtues or rectitude of newsgatherers any more than they were concerned with the theology preached by priests and ministers. What did concern them was the people's right to make up their own minds, freely, without controls, without someone deciding what they should or should not know.

In fact, I've always thought that it has been a mistake to describe the First Amendment in terms of either "separation of church and state" or "freedom of the press." These are really only different means to the same end. The end that is being sought *is the people's right to know*. That's what the First Amendment is all about. The people's right to choose for themselves what to believe, to hear every side, to weigh as much information and as many opinions as possible, to decide for themselves something as private as the way they pray and something as public as the size of the military budget.

James Madison put it this way: "A popular government," he wrote, "without popular information or the means of acquiring it, is but a prologue to farce or tragedy or perhaps both."

Of course, there are times when national security must be a consideration. But the real challenge in a democracy like ours is to limit these occasions as strictly as we can to ensure that the normal flow of facts and opinions is as open and as candid as we can humanly make them. Yet the recent trend is in the opposite direction. Increasingly, the emphasis is on what the people shouldn't know and the media shouldn't report. And I find it ironic that some of the advocates of these restrictions are the same people who, at least when it comes to the economy, speak about getting government off our backs. But when it comes to the free market of ideas and information, they seem to take an opposite tack, putting government on people's backs with its hands over their eyes.

Let me try to put this in a more concrete way. Whether we are liberals or conservatives, who in this room really believes that our information on some future military action that might involve us in another war should come solely from government forces? Who wants to make up his or her mind on the worth of the Strategic Defense Initiative or the safety of the space program only on the basis of what officials speaking for the government might choose to tell us? Who among us benefits from media that are constrained and intimidated, unable or afraid to seek out and report all of the information we need to decide intelligently on questions of the environment or the budget or social programs? I believe that it's in all of our interests to insist on the integrity of the First Amendment, not because we deny the human fallibility of the media, not because we believe its practitioners to be better or more informed than the rest of us, but because we care about our own freedom, our right to make up our own minds. Fifty years ago, in an attempt to satirize what he saw as the growing skepticism toward the Bill of Rights, H. L. Mencken rewrote the First Amendment to read: "There shall be complete freedom of speech and of the press subject to such regulations as the government or its agents may from time to time promulgate."

Unfortunately, in many countries of the world—in South Africa, in Chile, in the Soviet Union, in Nicaragua—that version of the First Amendment is fact rather than satire. In the United States, however, we still cling to the ideals set forth in our Constitution 200 years ago. Since then much in this country has changed. The small newspapers of the eighteenth century have given way to vast media networks that span this entire continent. The size and reach of our government has become immense. Our military and economic power is unmatched by any other nation.

In the future, technology will continue to revolutionize the way we gather and store and disseminate information. And yet the very basis of our freedom will continue to rest on the willingness to take the same risks that the Founders did. It's still a gamble. It always was and it always will be, but in the final analysis, it's the only way to preserve and to pass on that rich legacy that's been left to us.

2

The First Amendment—Its Current Condition

Craig R. Smith, Henry Geller, Patrick D. Maines, and Daniel L. Brenner

CRAIG R. SMITH

I thought in order to frame the beginning of this conference in some way that we might understand in a more cosmic sense that we might look at the evolution of technology, particularly communications technology, as it evolved in the Old World and as it has evolved in our world, in the New World. After that we should be able to move into microtechnologies with a better background.

Historically, in the Old World, there has always been a fear of new technology. That fear has led to the danger of regulation. My supposition is that the first time a guy walked up to the cave with fire, somebody ran over and poured a bucket of water on it. It was no doubt a committee decision. The same kinds of things probably happened with fireworks among the Chinese. There is a story that in England a bureaucrat proposed a law that no trains could go faster than 30 miles an hour because the wind would be sucked from the trains and people would suffocate. There has always been a concern for human safety that has led to certain kinds of regulation, and at times those regulations have been unseemly.

This is probably nowhere more true than in the world of information technology. As almost everyone knows, Johann Gutenberg introduced his Bible, put together with movable print, in 1456 in Mainz. There was an immediate reaction to this incredible breakthrough in technology because it would allow the wide dissemination of information very quickly. When Charles VII of France heard about it, he sent a man named Nicholas Jensen to Mainz to spy on it. Now this could have been the first instance of industrial espionage, but, in fact, it was not. King Charles wanted Jensen to tell him how this new device could be used to disseminate opinions about political thinking. Jensen became an apprentice to Gutenberg. King Charles was relieved to learn that government leaders imposed strict controls over what Gutenberg could publish.

It wasn't long afterward that controls began to be introduced throughout the Holy Roman Empire, Germany, and Austria. In 1485, for example, Archbishop Bertold von Hindenburg asked the town council of Frankfurt, which was nearby and maintained jurisdiction over Mainz, to censor all "dangerous publications." In 1486, Mainz and Frankfurt set up secular censorship boards to supplement the ecclesiastical boards that the archbishop had established. In 1579, the entire Frankfurt book market was put under the Imperial Censorship Commission which, again, complemented the ecclesiastical commission. The regular duties of these commissions were to suggest books that should be put on the Catholic Index of forbidden books to read. By 1750, the book fair of Frankfurt, which had been one of the great fairs of learning in all of Europe, had become a failure. While the presses in the Germanic provinces had cranked out 1,350 books in that year, only 42 German, 23 Latin, and 7 French titles were listed in the catalogue of the Frankfurt Fair because those were the only ones that the boards of Frankfurt, Mainz and the church approved for display at the fair.

Once censorship was established by the government, it spread to other institutions and other locations. Printing guilds themselves censored much of the work that came off the presses and often reported to the government that their publishers were printing tracts that were dangerous or seditious. They also turned tracts over to the church for review as they printed them.

The Council of the city of Basel in Switzerland suppressed the Koran until Martin Luther wrote a preface to it, an act significantly ahead of its time. Martin Luther begged that the Koran be published because, he said, it led to the greater glorification of God by all peoples. But the Germanic mania for discipline was most extreme in later periods. Even the philosopher G. W. Lyden in 1669 proposed making all book printers into government employees. And Metternich, in 1819, proposed centralization of the book trade under government control "to prevent the unlimited power of the booksellers who direct German public opinion."

Also in 1819, Karlsbad in Bohemia instituted censorship of all political pamphlets that were to be distributed. The culmination of this policy, and probably one of its worst results, came during the Third Reich when Hitler discovered a so-called fairness doctrine for newspapers. He used that doctrine to apply it to the electronic media. His minister of propaganda, Joseph

Goebbels, used this doctrine to create a monolithic media outlet for the Third Reich, and the results of which will go down in history.

I also want to look at England, because people tend to think of England as a little more enlightened than other places. The printing press came to England in 1476, 300 years before our revolution. The king at the time was Edward IV, and if you look up in an encyclopedia what was the most important thing to happen under Edward IV, you will find that it is normally considered to be the introduction of the printing press into England. The other important thing was that his death led to the War of the Roses. The Duke of Richmond united everyone under the House of Tudor and became Henry VII. Henry VII was not much more enlightened than some of his German predecessors when it came to the press. Using the excuse that the printing press might be used to print forged tidings, Henry VII began to institute controls. By the time of the accession of Henry VIII in 1538, all publications were subject to prior restraint; that is, they had to be reviewed by the Crown or the church before they could be published.

By 1585, the Stationers Company was granted a monopoly on publishing by royal decree. By 1630, when the Puritans set sail for America, there were only 23 master printers in all of England and only 55 presses were certified by the kingdom: 53 of them were in London under the watchful eye of the Crown, one of them was at Oxford, and one at Cambridge.

In 1642, a new law was passed. It was called the Act Preventing Abuses in Printing, Seditious, Unreasonable, and Unreliable Pamphlets and for Regulating Printing and the Presses." There followed a great outcry that led in 1644 to the publishing by John Milton of his *Areopagitica*. Milton called for a free press and celebrated the demise of the Star Chamber, which also used press laws to suppress all kinds of activities throughout the kingdom.

The printing press was a new technology both in England and in Germany. It was a new technology that disseminated information and political opinions and, therefore, was seen as quite dangerous. Regulations were imposed upon it.

The experience in the New World was quite different. In 1539, the first printing press was shipped to the Americas. It went to Mexico. Juan Cranberger of Seville sent the printing press, but it failed to attract enough interest to make much of a mark. It flourished later in the American colonies where there was a strong reaction to what had gone on in England. The first wave of settlers to come into New England feared the suppression of religious freedom. There was a desire not to follow the same path when it came to controlling printing presses in this country.

The first major case involving the printing press came in 1733—the case of John Peter Zenger. Zenger was charged with libel in the publication of his *New York Weekly Journal*. His attorney was Andrew Hamilton. Zenger was acquitted of libel on the principle that he told the truth. Truth was thus established as a defense in libel cases.

The printing press is also important in this country for a number of other reasons relating to communication among early patriots. In 1765, Patrick Henry made his historic Stamp Act speech protesting a new tax that had been imposed, not only on the press and the exchange of any kind of real estate paper, but on any transaction. This speech was distributed by underground presses throughout the colonies. Thomas Paine and the Sons of Liberty had been getting discouraged that a demand for independence was not growing in the colonies. When they read the speech by Patrick Henry, they were given new hope. They were moved to take new action toward independence; their tracts, their beliefs, were put into this press pipeline and sent throughout the thirteen colonies. When, for example, the Boston Massacre occurred in 1770, news of it spread throughout the colonies very quickly via the underground press.

When the Declaration of Independence was signed in 1776, it was published in most American newspapers, and that was also true of the newly proposed Constitution of 1787. The newspaper accounts of the Constitution and the constitutional debates served as a basis for the ratification conventions that took place in 1787 and 1788.

Pennsylvania had three elections leading up to its ratification convention, and in each one the Federalists, those in favor of the Constitution, won by two to one margins. At that convention, the anti-Federalists, noting that they were outnumbered two to one, thought that their best strategy was to introduce a Bill of Rights that would be appended to the Constitution. It is important that we understand that Pennsylvania had this early debate. In 1776, the colony of Pennsylvania created a document called the Pennsylvania Frame, which served as their constitution. The Pennsylvania Frame is the only document in 1776 to call for both freedom of speech and freedom of press. It served as a model for the Pennsylvania Ratification Convention. Pennsylvanians presented thirteen amendments that they wanted the constitution to have, including free press and free speech. Nine of those amendments became amendments to the Constitution in 1791 when the Bill of Rights was finally ratified. So it is at the Pennsylvania convention that the anti-Federalists begin to develop their strategy to demand, in exchange for ratification, a Bill of Rights, which became so important to the Constitution.

Now why was it in drafting the Constitution in 1787 that Hamilton and Madison and some of the others were not concerned about a Bill of Rights in the Constitution? Well, it is very clear from Madison's writing that he believed that if you enumerated rights in the Constitution, anything you left out would be assumed a power of the federal government. And because Madison couldn't name every single right, he thought it better to leave them all out and to say simply that what wasn't in the Constitution was left to the states and individual citizens. That did not go down well with the anti-Federalists. They were worried about the federal constitution becoming too strong. They did not trust Alexander Hamilton, and so in each of the ratification conventions they introduced a Bill of Rights, a strategy that had been initiated in the Pennsylvania Ratification Convention. It became the bargaining chip throughout.

One of the most important ratification conventions took place in June of 1788 in Virginia. Eight states had ratified the Constitution. At the time that Virginia's debate started, only one more state was needed to make the Constitution the law of the land. Thus the great burden of stopping this steamroller, of preventing the Constitution from being adopted fell on the anti-Federalists. One-fifth of all the rhetoric uttered at the Virginia Ratification Convention came from Patrick Henry. He dominated this convention, but failed to win his case because Madison had made a motion that the Constitution be considered clause by clause. The anti-Federalists had no alternative to the Constitution save the position that we must have a Bill of Rights. And so Virginia and a month later New York, by very close votes, ratified the Constitution. In fact, New Hampshire ratified four days before Virginia did but there was no way they could know about it. The Constitution became law, but there was a very strong feeling in this country that we needed a Bill of Rights, and among those rights were free speech and free press.

Now why was that the case? The press was not a new technology in this country, nor was public speaking. So there wasn't anything to fear about this technology. Second, the press had helped us gain our freedom from England, to break away from the Old World; and so the press was a friend to a lot of people in this country and they didn't want it controlled by the government. They had seen what had happened with licensing and monopolies and royal control in England. They demanded first and foremost a free press. George Mason, in Virginia's declaration of independence from England, had written that a free press was a bulwark of liberty. He had argued strongly for an amendment to the Constitution to protect it.

The new congress met in 1789 with James Madison a member of the House (because Patrick Henry wouldn't let him become a senator) and Alexander Hamilton in the Senate (because the Federalists and the merchants were dominating New York). They considered proposals for a Bill of Rights. More than 200 proposals came in, and the first group to take a crack at narrowing those proposals down and consolidating them was the House Committee headed by James Madison. At every point where one could amend the Constitution or amend these amendments to the Constitution, the First Amendment was strengthened. There was an attempt to limit it to political speech, and that was voted down. The bills then went over to the Senate where Hamilton's committee looked at them. There was an attempt to interpret the First Amendment to say all it should do is eliminate prior restraint. That was voted down. In fact, when the proposers went to the Senate and House Committees in conference to look at these documents and came up with the final thirteen that would be submitted to the states, they adopted the language that applied in the religious clause and combined the religious clause with free speech and free press. The result was the clause affirming that Congress "shall make no law abridging" freedom of speech or freedom of the press.

It is important to understand that legislative history. As Leonard Levy has admitted in his new book in 1985, in which he revised his old position, and what David Anderson from the University of Texas Law School writing in the UCLA *Law Review* has shown us is that the First Amendment was meant to have a much broader interpretation than has been given to it by legislatures and by the Congress and by the courts since. This theory is affirmed by legislative history and by a look at the newspapers that were extant at the time of the First Amendment. Why did we have the narrowing that took place after the First Amendment? Because judges were trained in Blackstone's commentaries, which were preoccupied with prior restraint. But clearly from this legislative history and from the notes we have from Madison, it is clear that the First Amendment was meant to protect more than just prior restraint and political speech.

The thirteen amendments were submitted to the states for ratification, and the first two were defeated. They concerned the election of members of the House and remuneration for members of the House of Representatives. So the Third Amendment became the first and the ten were added to the Constitution on December 15, 1791.

Over the course of our history, the First Amendment has had its ups and downs. For example, only seven years after ratification, the Alien and Sedition acts were hammered through the Congress by Alexander Hamilton. But the important thing to remember is that when the Alien and Sedition acts were passed, we were practically at war with France. The French had sunk 306 American ships. Imagine anyone doing that today and us not going to war with them. There was a great fear of subversion from the French Revolution, and that motivated the passage of the Alien and Sedition acts. They were used to put editors in jail for attacking President John Adams. Even a congressman went to jail. The acts were one of the major causes of the defeat of the Federalist party in 1800 when Jefferson became president of the United States. Jefferson quickly allowed the Alien and Sedition laws to lapse. The crises that have occurred with regard to the First Amendment have generally been connected with a fear of foreign power or a war. First Amendment rights were suppressed by Abraham Lincoln. They were suppressed by Franklin Roosevelt. And fear of subversion led to the McCarthy era. But out of each of those crises, the First Amendment has emerged stronger. Even today it is part of our civil religion.

One of the most important cases regarding the First Amendment was *Miami Herald v. Tornillo*. Pat Tornillo was running for public office in

Miami. The *Miami Herald* endorsed Pat Tornillo's opponent. Pat Tornillo found an obscure Florida law written in 1913 asking for equal space. His request was denied. The Florida Supreme Court upheld Pat Tornillo's position unanimously. That was appealed to the United States Supreme Court, which unanimously overruled the Florida Supreme Court, saying that the First Amendment means exactly what it says, and that even an equal space provision is a violation of the First Amendment. So when it comes to the print media in this country, we have protected it, we have made it sacrosanct because of our history.

The same is not the case with the electronic media. There we have not entirely broken away from the Old World. Broadcast stations are not only licensed, but the content of what they put on the air is controlled and their licenses can be taken away if that content does not please the Federal Communications Commission or other government agencies.

Today we're in the midst of an enormous battle over those content controls, and the rest of this conference is going to look at some of that technology and examine what is going on in the electronic media and how the First Amendment applies to it. As you go through the conference, I hope you will look at the history of the First Amendment in this country as it has been applied to the print media and ask yourself why if there are so many broadcast outlets in this country, so much electronic media, they have to suffer under content controls whereas the press does not.

HENRY GELLER

As you heard, there are three regulatory models. You've heard two of them. First, there is print under *Miami Herald v. Tornillo*: no governmental licensing or supervision. Second, there is broadcasting which Craig has mentioned, where you do have government licensing and scrutiny of overall programming efforts, including that mandated by the Fairness Doctrine. Incidentally, both of these models have been held to be constitutional. Craig mentioned *Miami Herald*, but *Red Lion* upheld unanimously the broadcast scheme as constitutional. In neither case is there any balancing; the court just makes its holding.

The third model, which Craig didn't mention but which is important here, is the common-carrier model. Print is often allied to this model: you send pamphlets or magazines through the postal service, a common carrier, and the telephone company renders the same kind of service. A 976 audio service can go out to anybody who wants to use this common-carrier method of distribution. I think, therefore, that the common carrier is of great importance.

As you just heard from Craig, there is a lot of criticism of the broadcast model. I think you'll hear more of it from the gentlemen very appropriately to my right. There's no question that the Fairness Doctrine or other aspects of broadcast regulation do have First Amendment strains. When the government intervenes in the process, it requires a tightrope walk, as the Supreme Court has said. But I'd like to give you some history in this area, broadcasting.

In the 1920s there was great chaos in broadcasting. Everybody would jump on everybody else's frequency. The result was no one could be heard. The broadcasters themselves said, "We need government licensing." The government, when it gives out something that is scarce, normally auctions it. If the government doesn't auction, it lets people run sheep on federal land with rentals. The government didn't do either here. Instead, Congress said, "We will give the frequency free on condition that the broadcaster use it as a fiduciary for all those who are kept off, because the crucial consideration is that more people want to broadcast than there are available frequencies." And to answer Craig's question now, that's still true today. If you opened a VHF channel in San Diego, you'd have a dozen applicants for it. In Los Angeles, a station passed hands for $510 million, the assets maybe were $40 million, and the rest a piece of paper representing the government license. Since there are still more people that want to broadcast than available channels, the government still has to license, so the broadcaster, when he accepts the license, is taking it as fiduciary for those who are kept off. That is the reason you have this public trustee licensing scheme. The broadcaster is then required to do local programming. That's why San Diego has channels as against Los Angeles. The allocation scheme calls for it. If you don't get local programming, you've undermined the allocations scheme. The same thing is true as to informational programming. Broadcasting has an enormous chunk of the spectrum as against common carrier, private radio, and so on, because of the contribution it can make to an informed electorate. And finally, if you are a fiduciary, you clearly have to have a Fairness Doctrine, because if you don't, if you only put on the views you agree with, you're not a fiduciary, it's your private property and it should have been auctioned.

Now the argument is made that the Fairness Doctrine is chilling. I think it's exaggerated. The large broadcasters, the networks are not chilled at all. They don't pay attention to it, don't even know it exists. The small broadcaster has to hire an attorney to handle complaints, and there it could be chilling. The smaller broadcaster doesn't want to be controversial anyway, for the most part.

But I want to stress again: There is no such thing as a surgical strike on the Fairness Doctrine. If you eliminate that doctrine, the entire scheme of public trustee licensing will unravel. Equal time will go. The Supreme Court said the two are equivalent in *Red Lion*. Judge Bork just said it in a recent opinion when he was called upon to invalidate equal time; he said, "I can't do that. The Supreme Court in *Red Lion* said that it's the same as fairness for constitutional purposes." And, you will eliminate entirely all this public trustee licensing. There was a station in Jackson, Mississippi. It was run by a racist in the early 60s. All he would present was the White Citizens Council, never the blacks who composed 45 percent of his listening audience. He lost his station finally. But under the new concept espoused by the FCC, he would be renewed as a public fiduciary. That's absurd. So what I'm saying to you here is that if the broadcasters succeed, the entire compact that has been made over sixty years will unravel and you will have to get to auctions or spectrum usage fees.

Now I've been talking constitutional law. As a matter of policy, if that happened, I would not be unhappy. The reason why is not the First Amendment strains, although they're there; it's because the regulation has been very ineffectual. It's been ineffectual from the very beginning. Today it is the most ineffectual it has ever been. The former chairman of the commission, Mark Fowler, has called television a toaster with pictures and acts upon that basis. The commission renews licenses with only a postcard. It doesn't have the least notion of any programming information. It relies upon the public. But ask yourself how many times you go out and monitor a station or go look at what a station has done in the way of public service. So what we have is ineffectual regulation and I would eliminate it. First in radio, and if it worked in radio, I would eliminate it in television. But I would eliminate it for a price. Remember, the broadcasters volunteered to be public trustees. If somebody got on their channel in radio, they would run to the government and say enjoin them, stop them. That's not true of print. So that what you need here is money, and I would exact a usage fee and use it to support public broadcasting. I would then have a structure that worked for me instead of the present regulatory structure, which does not. If it worked in radio, I'd move on to television.

The reason you can't get such a structure is not Congress. Congress is willing to do it in radio. The reason is the broadcaster, who loves being called a public trustee as long as it's not enforced , and it is the National Association of Broadcasters (NAB) who have stopped all progress.

Let me turn very briefly to cable. Cable represents a very difficult and very interesting issue under the First Amendment. It carries broadcast signals and is enmeshed with the broadcast system so that you can do broadcast regulation as to that aspect. You have to make a reasonable regulation, but in my view a cable system in Riverton, Wyoming, cannot import Denver signals and not carry the local station. If the local station's cut off from its viewers, and goes off the air, thousands of people in farmhouses would then lose their only service. That's one aspect.

Cable itself, however, originates programming using the satellite. Dick Munro was too modest last night. He really made this revolution that has occurred here when he turned with HBO to the use of the satellite. Now as to that type of operation by cable, I think they are telepublishers and they come under *Miami Herald* V. *Tornillo*. There should be no regulation by the local franchising authority or by the FCC or any other body of the content of their program.

But cable also gets a franchise from the city. It needs that franchise in order to do business, to use the streets, and that franchise turns out to result in a very limited number of operations. Technically, you are not going to have a wall of wires going down the streets. And as a matter of economics, you're going to end up with only one or two, either monopoly or duopoly, and most likely monopoly. That's the subject for the next panel so I won't go on to it. So what you have is the government giving out a franchise that is necessary to do a mass media business and it turns out to be a monopoly or duopoly. In those circumstances a government can provide what is called diversification, the *Associated Press* principle. The underlying assumption of the First Amendment is that the American people receive information from diverse and antagonistic sources. If the cable entity controls the content of all 74 channels, that goes against diversification. So I believe the government can step in and not just focus on the right of the speaker, the cable entrepreneur, but for diversification purposes on the right of the listener. The government wants to free up 10 percent to 15 percent of cable's channel capacity for public access channels or lease channel, and I think that will be held to be constitutional. But that also is now being fought out. We don't know the answer to that. It comes under a doctrine called *O'Brien*, which I don't have time to develop. And what I've told you reflects the policy of the Congress and the Cable Act of 1984. It's rather imperfect but it is there.

PATRICK D. MAINES

As was indicated in my introduction, the Media Institute is a nonprofit media research foundation headquartered in Washington that gets its support from a wide range of corporations and foundations including, most important, a growing number of media companies ranging from newspaper companies to broadcasting companies to cable companies and phone companies.

In recent years the Media Institute has gotten involved in a great many different kinds of activities, but the one activity that's particularly germane to this gathering is our work in the area of the new media technologies and the First Amendment. Although some related activities preceded the formation of it, the Institute has been involved with the First Amendment most actively just since January of this year when we created a program entity called the First Amendment Center for the New Media. This name does not suggest any animus on our part with respect to the old media, it's just that the old media are better understood and have their defenders. The new media are less well understood and have few defenders and a lot of critics.

Merely to list some of the activities the First Amendment Center has gotten involved in is to illustrate what we think of the current status of the First Amendment. We were one of six organizations that filed comments with the FCC seeking repeal of the Fairness Doctrine. We filed a Friend of the Court Brief in an important, although difficult, cable case, siding with the cable company in the argument that it traduces the First Amendment for a community to allow only one cable franchise. We are likely to get involved shortly in yet another cable case in which we will argue that it is unconstitutional for cities to mandate public access channels for cable systems.

We have copublished, with the Freedom of Expression Foundation, a book that looks broadly at content controls on the electronic media, and specifically at videotext. We don't think there should be any.

And finally, and maybe most controversially, we have just recently filed as an intervenor in Judge Green's *Triennial Review*. Our position is that it is unconstitutional to prohibit the Bell Operating Companies (BOC) from offering information services in their local service areas. I should add that there's a strong chance that we'll be filing again as intervenors in the appeal phase of this important case.

Before I get into the substance of my remarks, one more preliminary observation. The panelists in this session don't agree about all things. But I think they do agree about a *few* things, and I'd like to name those things. I think they agree that, even though they may interpret it a little differently, the First Amendment is a good idea. I think they agree that the First Amendment has a continuing importance, that it isn't just some relic of another age. And I think that they all believe that as this country is in the midst of a vast and underreported communications revolution, that it's terribly important that the people, like you, become better informed and more actively involved in these kinds of matters. In the end, what we're talking about here is what kind of environment will exist for you to get news and information, and on the other hand, what kind of an environment there will be for you to produce and distribute news and information.

What is the current condition of the First Amendment? In my opinion, the First Amendment, as it is applied to the electronic media, is in a very parlous state. One sees that everywhere. In broadcasting, the Fairness Doctrine is about to be resurrected from the dead. And that's a mistake. In the matter of cable TV, despite some lovely cases being fought and won here in California, primarily by this maverick attorney Harold Farrow, the cable industry continues to be regulated extensively by local and federal governments. In remote-sensing, there are phony national security concerns that are frustrating not only the development of a news gathering source, but particularly of an American news gathering source. In information services, there have been attempts to reclassify and to deny access to government and private data bases, again on national security grounds. And in telephony, as I mentioned earlier, there continues to be an attempt to deny phone companies the right to act as speakers. So I'd say in conclusion that I think that the First Amendment is sort of up for grabs, and is by no means an assured concept.

DANIEL L. BRENNER

Let me try to sketch out what I think is the condition of the First Amendment. I think we need to remind ourselves of the majesty of the First Amendment, why it is so important. Many of us feel this intuitively when we travel to countries that don't have a First Amendment tradition, if you go as I did last summer to East Berlin. While the streets superficially look very much like those of the West (indeed there are hotels that look identical to this Marriott), the place where freedoms are housed is entirely different. There just isn't the same freedom. You cannot say the same things on streets or in pamphlets or on radio or TV. Go to England. There you will find a State Secrets Act. In the United States we have no State Secrets Act. There is no law that, by itself, prohibits the publication of state secrets in this country. You may be surprised to learn that, but that's the reality of this country. We are a remarkably free country.

If you hang out at an airport for longer than you'd like, you will soon meet people who would like you to sign a petition sending Jane Fonda to Hanoi or offer you a complementary helping of whale meat. That, too, is the First Amendment, and it annoys us sometimes, and it irritates us, and it takes up our time. But that is a tradition of freedom of expression, and that is what differentiates this country from almost any other country in the world—the breadth of our First Amendment.

Well, what is the goal of the First Amendment? Why are we here? Why are we venerating this particular provision of our Constitution? No one's quite sure. The U.S. Supreme Court does not endorse a singular purpose of the First Amendment.

For a long time, it was argued that the First Amendment was really designed to protect political speech. This, indeed, is the issue that got Judge Robert H. Bork into some trouble this summer. In 1971 he argued that only political speech was protected by the First Amendment, following the tradition of the earlier writings of Alexander Meiklejohn. But we know that is not enough. Entertainment can be not only an amusement, but educational, too. That, too, deserves protection, even though it may not relate directly to a political issue.

Remember that the First Amendment protects self-expression, the right of people to express their own ideas. Those ideas may have nothing to do with anything political or may even be totally nonsensical, as far as we can determine. But that expression may be the germ of an idea for that individual. It could be that that germ will some day lead to important cultural or intellectual or political awareness. We are celebrating the twentieth anniversary of the Beatles' Sergeant Pepper album. There's a great deal that that album had to say about the United States and the human condition that wasn't going to be printed on the front page of the local paper. So the First Amendment also protects individual self-fulfillment because we as human beings want to express ourselves, whether it's by wearing bow ties from time to time or writing free-verse poetry. The point is, we're free to do these things, and we cherish that freedom in this country. So, although there is no one grand unifying First Amendment theory in our country, at least this is true: government does not have a monopoly on the truth. Whenever the government tries to say, "No, you can't say something," or "No, *you* may speak for what is right and true but *others* will be excluded," we get concerned. It's not because we believe the truth will emerge from this cacophony of ideas. It may or may not. We may take 20 years to find out what's true. But the idea is, the government doesn't know what's right all the time. This is the principle we want to protect in interpreting our First Amendment.

Judge Learned Hand said it perhaps better than anyone: "The First Amendment presupposes that right conclusions are more likely to be gathered out of the multitude of tongues than through any kind of authoritative selection." So at least we know this: government ought not to be picking and choosing what's true.

This leads to a very broad understanding of the First Amendment. What isn't covered by the First Amendment? Is it a First Amendment matter, for example, to choose between Lee jeans and Levis? If you think that's a facetious question, ask kids what's really important in their lives, and it's probably the label on the clothes that they wear. That's probably where they demonstrate the most self-expression and where they get hurt the most when they can't pursue it.

Most First Amendment law is a twentieth-century phenomenon. Starting with the espionage cases out of World War I, we developed the First Amendment on one side and First Amendment values on the other, closely linked but not quite the same thing. Former U.S. Supreme Court Justice Potter Stewart said this: "If I've exaggerated, it is only to make clear the dangers that beset us when we lose sight of the First Amendment itself and march forth in blind pursuit of its 'values.'" So we want to distinguish between First Amendment values that are important but not the same thing as what the amendment ought to protect.

Well, what does the amendment specifically protect? Here we get into a distinction between speech and press. Believe it or not, the Supreme Court has not told us whether or not the freedom of speech and of press are overlapping. Some judges, Justice Stewart in particular, believe that the press clause is different from the speech clause. He wrote that the press clause was meant to protect an industry. By doing so we protect the right of people to receive information.

But the court has not always interpreted the press and the speech clause differently. That is to say, the press has not always been given special protection. If a reporter is subpoenaed by a grand jury, that reporter is not given any special protection against testifying or producing documents because he or she happens to work for a newspaper or a television station. If a reporter wants to visit a prison to report on prison conditions or interview a prisoner, there is no special right of a reporter to go into prison. So we have to realize that the court has not always said that the press is entitled to some special protection. On the other hand in defamation we know, ever since *New York Times* v. *Sullivan,* that the press is given a breathing space for errors in regard to libel.

Or consider the problem of, who is the press? Let's say we define ourselves as freelance writers. We want to get a press pass to cover some event. Are we entitled to the same press credentials that the *Los Angeles Times* is? That the partisan press, the *National Review,* is? How do you make those distinctions? How should the government make those decisions? Those are some of the hard questions that arise in just defining who the press is?

Let me turn in the remaining minutes to how the courts classify the different kinds of laws under the First Amendment. At the risk of oversimplifying somewhat, on the one hand you have content-related laws, laws that suppress ideas. An example: There used to be a law in New York that said you couldn't advocate adultery. It was just a forbidden act. Well, if any of you have ever read *Lady Chatterley's Lover,* you know very well that the book does not exactly condemn adultery. And in a case called *Kingsley International Pictures* v. *Board of Regents,* the court said you cannot ban an idea. No idea is forbidden under the Constitution. So the suppression of content-related messages, laws that identify certain points of view, undergo the strictest scrutiny by the court. The court says you can't have such laws, generally speaking.

There are other kinds of laws affecting speech, laws that are content neutral. Not all content-neutral laws are constitutional, but since they do not discriminate on viewpoint, they are more likely to be upheld. The classic example: a city says you can't have sound trucks near a hospital. It doesn't care whether you are prosocialist or antisocialist, you just can't have sound trucks near a hospital. Well, in fact, those kind of laws can affect those people who use sound trucks, say Iranian protesters with generally low-financed political speech. But we generally view such a law as content neutral.

So, as we examine regulations during this conference, are they content-related laws or content neutral?

Take the case of cable TV's First Amendment rights and franchising. The act of franchising is essentially a content-neutral act. Say one is denied a franchise in a competitive bidding situation. People are not denied franchises because of what they want to say. No one is saying, "Oh, you want to say something positive about the Sandinistas, that's why we're denying you a franchise." That is not the issue in these cases. But regulating the content of HBO or CNN based on what is said—that is content-related.

I hope that you'll think of these two issues as we go through this day: One is remembering what it is that the First Amendment is about. It's about the suppression of viewpoints and our country's utter contempt of government attempts to suppress viewpoints. You know, great First Amendment cases have often involved nonmainstream plaintiffs, those who do not express a majoritarian standpoint. The Scientologists are probably the leading First Amendment litigants in the United States today. The right to pass out leaflets, to express different viewpoints, to resist government efforts to control speech—these are the people shaping individual rights. I'm surprised that the American Civil Liberties Union isn't represented at this conference because that group fights for preserving the right to hear viewpoints outside of the mainstream.

Second, it is important to remember what the First Amendment discussions should be about, which is the flip side of my other point: to avoid trivializing the First Amendment. I think Patrick Maines makes a very good point, that in this debate over new technologies that we do not use the First Amendment where it doesn't fit, where it doesn't belong. Industries should not use the First Amendment as a battering ram to make an economic point where other issues are really far more significant. So, for example, if somebody is denied a cable TV franchise and it's really a due process violation where the city council is corrupt, let's call it what it is, corruption of the process. Let's not try to append the First Amendment as some sort of global gloss on the whole process.

I think if we keep those two things in mind, we will avoid the backlash that can come when you magnetize all of the law into one big First Amendment question. You know, not everything involving the media does involve the First Amendment. Many things do. The Fairness Doctrine does. Content regulation of broadcasting does. Content regulation of cable does. Attempts to control electronic information flow that is content-related does. But not every issue does, and I think that's the difference.

OPEN DISCUSSION

Moderator: Now there'll be a kind of open discussion and we'll let any panelist, if he will hold his comments or questions to two minutes, respond to another panelist's earlier statement.

Smith: Let me do it in sixty seconds if I can. I was limited in the amount of time I have normally for a 90-minute lecture, but to help you with

Henry's point, if you look at 1949, you can find the promulgation of the Fairness Doctrine is listed. Like a fork, it has two prongs. First, broadcasters are required to cover controversial issues, and second, they must provide an opportunity for presentation of contrasting views. In 1969, the *Red Lion* decision to which Henry referred was supported unanimously. In 1984, another Supreme Court decision says maybe we ought to look again at the *Red Lion* decision. Going back and using the standards on which that decision was based, we may find some question with regard to the scarcity rationale and the chilling effect of the Fairness Doctrine. So I just wanted to point that out on the list of things I asked to be distributed. You can find a quick read into what we're referring to when we talk about the Fairness Doctrine.

Moderator: Thank you. Any other?

Geller: I just want to say very quickly that there's complete agreement about the importance of the First Amendment; that you shouldn't have suppression of viewpoint, it should be content-neutral. Also unlike Patrick, I think the situation is going to get better, that we're moving to the telephone company with a broadband fiber into the home, and we will therefore get to the print model, video publishing over common carrier. I just want to add to Dan's presentation that the First Amendment does apply differently with different media. The Supreme Court has stressed that, and you can see the need to apply it in a content-neutral way. Just take a telephone company. Suppose General Telephone or Pacific Bell said that "Yes, we're going to render telephone service, but we'd like to control the content of every message that goes into the home." They're not allowed to do that. A telephone company has to have separation of content and conduit on the vast majority of its operation, and everybody would sustain that as promoting the First Amendment.

When you get to cable you get the same thing. You want to allow the cable entity, because it's not a telephone company, to control 85 percent to 90 percent. But again, in a content-neutral fashion when you're giving a franchise, since you are in telephone, since it results in this type of bottleneck, to free 10 percent to 15 percent for leased access I believe is permissible, just the way it is to free 99 percent in the case of the telephone company.

For one final example take the newspaper. The most precious of all things we've been talking about—to be a First Amendment broadcast speaker—is not allowed if a daily newspaper wants to own a TV station in the same area. It isn't allowed because people get their news from newspapers and television. The Supreme Court has unanimously approved that, saying it's a content-neutral regulation that promotes the Associated Press principle I told you about, the underlying assumption of the First Amendment. So all I'm saying is while we all agree how precious the First Amendment is, it doesn't mean that there's no government regulation in this area, that there's nothing the government can do that won't promote the First Amendment.

Moderator: Rebuttal or comment?

Maines: I'm not quite sure I know where to begin, but let's be concrete about one thing. Let's talk about cable TV for one minute. Cable TV should be likened to the print model, not the broadcast model. Cable TV doesn't traffic in a scarce electromagnetic spectrum. It's a privately owned cable. Cable TV, however, suffers a good deal of regulation, regulation that is, in fact, significantly greater than that of the broadcasters. Let me give you one example.

Imagine that the city council here in San Diego were to decide to make the San Diego newspapers more "representative," to operate them more in the "public interest," and that they required, for instance, that the *San Diego Union* run not just letters to the editor, but that they set aside a page or two for opinions or articles or news stories written by whoever got there first. You could call it the "public access" page. The city council might demand additionally that governmental information come straight from the source, that is from governmental agencies, without going through a filter of an independent editorial process, and might refer to that as the "institutional" requirement. To complete the picture, imagine that the council required that newspapers not discriminate against small, suburban papers that have limited circulation, and so demanded that some section of the dominant newspaper be given over to reprinting in its pages sections of other, smaller newspapers, calling this the "must-carry" obligation. Well, clearly, if this set of proposals were made by anybody's city council it would be thrown out. It would be laughable. Yet precisely these kinds of things are currently happening to cable TV. Mandated "public access," "institutional loops," and "must carry" of broadcast signals are everyday realities in the life of this country's cablecasters. Let me add one more thing to this discussion of cable and the First Amendment. I think it is unconstitutional, that it traduces the First Amendment, for cities to award a single cable franchise, and I think so because I think it denies the right to speak to would-be cable operators.

Moderator: Let me ask Dan if he wants to respond to that.

Brenner: Yeah, Glen you may just want to take a seat, this is going to take a little while. (Laughter) I spent my summer vacation trying to answer the question that Patrick has just posed. It is a complicated answer. But I think it starts from what I expressed a little earlier: keep your eye on what the First Amendment protects. It involves many things, and there are areas where the First Amendment is not content-related, but where it does have an effect. Not all content-neutral regulation is constitutional. It's a question of the standard that you apply, the degree of scrutiny, as the court would say; or, for nonlawyers, how wide you open your eyes at the text before you say this is offensive as a constitutional matter. That exercise is less for content-neutral regulation. Your eyes dilate a bit when it's content-related and your pupils contract when it's not. At least that is sort of the way the court has developed the doctrine.

Now, your example about a newspaper being subject to all of these requirements avoids a couple of things. Newspapers do not make nontransient uses of city streets.

Maines: What is nontransient?

Brenner: Newspapers do not require dedicated street space, pole space, air space in order to undertake their business.

Maines: No, but they put their vending machines on the street, they haul their newspapers to homes and on streets.

Brenner: Now let's separate those two. When they use the streets to move papers, it's one thing. They get on and they get off, it's transient. From time immemorial, to quote *Hague* V. *CIO*, that has been a function of city streets. When newspapers put in permanent vending courts government can regulate the placement of those racks. Newspapers can be charged a fee for placing those racks. In the *Gannett* case in New York, newspapers were being charged a fee for racks and were not being allowed to place them anywhere they liked in the subway corridors. And the court said, that's right.

Maines: What's your point?

Brenner: My point is, if a cable system asks a city to dedicate rights-of-way on a nontransient or permanent basis, that is a demand other media have not made. That begins to open the question, I think, of what the city can seek in return for granting that nontransient use. Even more significant, there's an economic matter. Not only does the cable get the nontransient use, but the city goes ahead and says we will make sure you get all the easements you need in order to construct your cable system. Getting those easements could be the hardest thing about building a cable system. Let's say you want to go out in San Diego and become a cable TV operator and the city said fine, here's your license, go ahead. Now you get to the first private piece of property that we need to cross. The owner says, well, I'd be delighted to have you operate a cable system if you'll pay me 10 percent of the value of your system. You say, wait a second. The difference is the city can, through its eminent domain power, make it possible for the cable system to be built, for access to private property to be acquired through the state.

Maines: It can and it does.

Brenner: Okay, but that's different from a newspaper, which doesn't ask the city to lend it that kind of muscle. It doesn't ask the city in a sense to negotiate all of those rights for it. It makes only nontransient use of space that from time immemorial has been used for speech—streets and sidewalks. That is the difference. Now I didn't say it was decisive. I don't say the book is closed, but I think there is a difference.

Maines: You really have better points to make than this one. Why don't you make the one . . . ?

Brenner: Well, you're not Kreshkin, because I thought I just made my big point.

Maines: I don't think so.

Brenner: All right, then, let me add what I consider the coups de grace. Or for those of you who had dessert last night, the whipped cream on the— what was that—parfait. One of the real questions. A colleague of mine describes it as ice cream with curry. Granted, you and I have probably an honest disagreement as to the weight to be given to some of the other arguments that are made on behalf of *City v. Cable*. I agree, for example, the naturally monopoly question is hardly obvious. People argue that you can only have one cable system, cable's a natural monopoly; ergo, you can only license one. I will concede that is not clearly a fact. And I will also concede that the degree of aesthetic blight and traffic patterns raised by a second cable system construction is an open question. Courts are faced with a very difficult challenge. We have district court judges here in California who aren't attending seminars like this, who don't think about the media all day long, and who are being asked to decide whether franchising is constitutional, whether access is constitutional. These, in my mind, are related and are part of complicated balancing of First Amendment interests. Access provides excluded speakers the right to speak on cable. It exists in no other media. If I lose a franchise battle, I can still speak in cable through access. All of these rules were part of the Cable Act of 1984 where Congress considered the views of many voices on the issue, the cities, the cable industry. Indeed, the act was essentially a compromise with some input from Congress and public interest groups, particularly on the access question. If there's something wrong in this area, fundamentally wrong, given this balance, isn't the right way for this country to proceed through the legislative process? Should courts, in a sense, cherry pick the act for this piece they don't like and that piece they don't like, when those different pieces might have been part of an over all balance that Congress tried to achieve in this act? I think it's risky business for a trial court to start taking apart content-neutral regulations that are part of an overall package. Instead, I think they should defer to Congress's judgment in this area, so long as there is no evidence of suppression. And there is generally no evidence of viewpoint suppression in exclusive licensing. On the other hand, if there's no access right in cable, then the excluded franchise applicant cannot speak on cable as of right. This is one instance where I think the act could be unconstitutional, where a city has granted only one license and has no access for excluding speakers. Such content-neutral regulation might leave no adequate alternative, although an excluded operator could still speak a leaflet as she pleases. Where the city has granted a franchise through perceived corruption of the process, as was the case apparently in Sacramento, there's certainly a problem with that grant. I don't think it's a First Amendment problem. I think it's a due process problem. It doesn't mean that grant should be approved, but the solution is not to declare franchising unconstitutional.

Smith: Mr. Brenner, we're talking about the First Amendment as it is now, and I'm going to ask a question that pertains I think to the lives of some of us as they are now. Advertising and television could create Spuds MacKenzie. Part of marketing includes selling of T-shirts. We have a case in North San Diego County in which high schools have banned T-shirts that advertise Corona Beer or Spuds MacKenzie, and the kids have taken that to court apparently. We'll see what happens there. I talked to some elementary school educators recently and they say they're confronting the issue of Spuds MacKenzie T-shirts on elementary school kids, and they don't like them wearing those shirts, but Spuds is real cute. He doesn't say drunken animal, he says party animal. I wonder what the panel thinks about this kind of television influence on our kids. And do elementary school kids have First Amendment rights? *Tinker* v. *Des Moines* says when you wear a black armband protesting the Vietnam War, you don't leave your First Amendment rights at the schoolhouse door, but do you if you're wearing the Spuds MacKenzie T-shirt and you're an elementary school kid?

Moderator: Dan, do you want to respond to that?

Brenner: I think you've raised an important question. If you ask a seven-year-old what's important, it is exactly that Spuds MacKenzie shirt. That goes to this goal of self-fulfillment that the First Amendment arguably protects. Now, whether they have the right to violate somebody's commercial... if Spuds MacKenzie is copyrighted to Anheuser Busch, I don't care if you're a seven-year-old or seventy-year-old, you have no right to steal someone's copyright. The First Amendment doesn't protect the theft of the Spuds MacKenzie logo.

Smith: Kids are buying the shirts.

Brenner: And just buying them and being told they can't wear. . . .

Smith: The administration is saying that you can't wear these shirts to school.

Brenner: That is a core First Amendment issue. That is suppression of a viewpoint. Now to us, it's an absolute idiotic viewpoint. It's a stupid, beer-selling dog. But to these children, it may be the best way they can articulate what freedom is about. This is, the right to be free, the right to enjoy the sort of delirious state that those commercials portray. Now you and I may say it's stupid and it's unhealthy, but it's the same thing that they were criticizing my generation for as to rock music and rock'n roll music for ten years before.

Smith: No, but the point they make is they don't want the kids in a delirious state during school, as you're describing. They didn't want you playing rock music in the classroom or while the teacher was trying to teach.

Brenner: Was that the issue? I don't think so. Officials didn't want my generation to wear long hair and they didn't want people fifteen years ahead of me to wear grease-backed hair. And I think it is important, at least in my view of the First Amendment, that self-fulfillment be part of the First Amendment's protection.

Smith: I have two questions. One is an access question, and the analogy I like to use relates to a regulation that a city might impose on a bookstore that would specify or require that a bookstore devote 15 percent of its shelf space to books and publications by local authors, let's say. It seems to me that's very similar to a cable access requirement. And that promotes diversity, promotes localism in those First Amendment values. Would that kind of thing be constitutional? And would it make a difference? Mr. Geller, let's say the city also had a requirement that any bookstore in the city be a minimum number of square feet, and that was so large that as an economic matter you'd only have one bookstore. And, Dan, to get to your point about nontransient use of public facilities, what if this law only applied to bookstores that were in the lobbies of government buildings? That's making a nontransient use of a public facility. Would it therefore be constitutional?

Geller: The answer is that none of those regulations that were mentioned would be constitutional as applied to a bookstore or a newspaper. I concede that. That was the exact argument that was made to the court in the "must carry" argument incidentally two weeks ago. The difference is that cable does get a franchise to use the streets. That franchise is necessary to carry out its mass media business. It turns out that franchise is a monopoly or duopoly, and that on that basis the government can do diversification under *O'Brien*. It's a substantial governmental interest. The burden is incidental, it's not meant to suppress anything, and it's no more than essential to carry out. I think the government can do it. I think they can do it for the same reason that you could do access in broadcasting. We'll just have to wait and see what the Supreme Court holds because that's the only opinion that matters. But there's a big distinction between what cable does and how cable operates. The sine qua non of cable operation is obtain a franchise to use the city's streets, and that franchise is very limited, and that's not what a bookstore does and that's not what a newspaper does.

Smith: I guess where Patrick and I might be coming down on this is that if you said, look, whatever you have to do to get the license, or whatever you have to do to lay cable to provide a quality signal that meets the market demand in this area, is fine with us. But when you start adding things to those provisions that then carry over, not only in terms of your technological quality and meeting the market demand, but get into areas which say the content of this will be judged by us, the city council, or the FCC, then you are on very dangerous ground, in danger of violating the First Amendment.

Moderator: Let me take our last question from this gentleman here.

Smith: I'd like to toss in another issue for the model, and that is the distinction between private communication and broadcasts. Private communication in the sense that it is definitely from one person to another specific individual or perhaps from a person to an organization or from an organization to another organization. It is definitely a targeted communication as contrasted with a broadcast communication where an individual or organization formulates a message and puts it out to whoever might choose to tune in. So there are the issues of the broadcaster and the issues of the listener, the right of access to tune in to different views.

Brenner: Why does that make a difference under the First Amendment?

Smith: Well, it seems to me that in this spectrum that goes from a definite me to you, embracing only two individuals, on the one hand to the broadest sense of let's say an organization broadcasting to an unknown public, to anyone who chooses to tune in, on the other, somewhere in that spectrum, of course, First Amendment issues come in. And one key issue that I see in the new technologies, let's see if I can formulate this succinctly, given the rapid increase of bandwidth that is available from airwaves to cables to fibers so that we could have essentially infinite bandwidth available, it would be very easy for me to say I, as an individual—there's one other ingredient—not only bandwidth but personal technology to receive and interpret—personal computers, personal video broadcasting, so that it is easily possible for an individual to set up his or her own TV station for both broadcast and reception.

Moderator: Do you want someone to respond to these points?

Smith: What I'm getting at is we're going to have a muddle. Where does the government step in when each of us is a broadcaster and each of us is a receiver, and we can essentially create our own newspaper or our own television station and target our subscribers?

Brenner: Let me just suggest one guidepost or Rosetta stone. It also relates to the cable area. Maybe the First Amendment is most keenly concerned with protecting the conscious expression of an individual. Other things are also protected. After all, newspaper editors don't read everything that's in their newspaper, but we expect it should be protected. On the other hand, is there a difference between someone who is saying what they personally have written or believe and someone—a cable operator, telephone company, whoever—who's broadcasting or carrying, shall I say, 100 different messages? Cox Cable San Diego brings you these 100 cable channels. But nobody in the Cox organization knows what's being carried on any but perhaps one or two of the channels. Is that First Amendment activity or are they doing something else?

Smith: I would like to interject. If I publish my own corporate newsletter, I can now publish it either in paper or in video and distribute it as widely as the *Los Angeles Times*.

Geller: And you continue to do it under a print model. You may use common carriers who have to make their services available indifferently, but when videotext comes and other technologies come, they will be under a print model.

Brenner: That's not necessarily true. The court of appeals has ruled in

T.R.A.C. v. *FCC* that the FCC could impose a Fairness Doctrine on teletext and videotext.

Moderator: We are out of time on this first panel discussion. Let's hear a warm and hearty thanks for all these people.

3

The First Amendment—Forces of Change

Richard M. Schmidt, Jr., John Redpath, Jr.,
Lee Burdick, Edward T. Reilly, Jr., and
Henry Geller

RICHARD M. SCHMIDT, JR.

I couldn't help but think when I was listening to the previous panel that I have a friend in Washington, a retired United Press journalist, who has always contended that the founding fathers were really not as bright as a lot of us thought when they drafted the First Amendment. He said, if you stop and think about it, we would have been better off if they put a period after "Congress shall make no law." And I think that was sort of the thrust of what we just heard from the born-again regulators headed by Henry Geller who isn't quite sure what he wants to regulate.

The late Chief Justice of the United States, Earl Warren, stated in a speech that he didn't think the First Amendment would be adopted in Bicentennial America, and that may be true. I certainly hope not. Henry and I served on the Commission on Freedom and Equality of Access to Information of the American Library Association in 1983. We struggled for about two years looking at the new technologies. We realized then as we do now that our nation's basic policies and institutions for disseminating information were formed, obviously, in the era of print dominance. Freedom of information was defined as freedom of press, and print literacy was the key for acquiring information. Keeping in mind the James Madison quote that Dick Munro gave us last night about knowledge will forever govern ignorance, I think that is the basis from which most of us have worked. You must realize that the Bill of Rights and the information of that era came through written pamphlets and broadsides, through single-sheet weekly newspapers, preachers speaking from pulpits, and orators in court house squares.

By the end of the nineteenth century, the technology for disseminating information had changed dramatically. High speed presses and mechanical production of paper dramatically lowered the cost of print and made possible the penny paper, the dime novel, and the mass market magazine. Telegraph lines started instantaneous communication of news across the country, and the creation of rail and telegraph networks enormously broadened the access of the American public to information.

Then, following World War I, we saw two technological developments develop into mass media: motion pictures and radio. And in the same tradition our courts have often been slow to catch up and interpret the role of the First Amendment in new technologies, and I submit they are just as slow today in doing so.

Craig Smith mentioned the case of *Miami Herald* v. *Tornillo*. I served as co-counsel in that case on behalf of the *Miami Herald* and the Supreme Court of the United States. We were absolutely petrified as to how we were going to distinguish the *Red Lion* case from our factual situation. Incidentally, Craig referred to it as an obscure Florida statute. I wish it had been. It was adopted back in 1923. Occasionally somebody would come in and demand that this statute, which mandated equal access for candidates, be enforced, and the attorney general of Florida, whoever he was at that particular time, would say, no, it's unconstitutional. Finally, Pat Tornillo found an attorney general who was willing to take it to court. He found a supreme court in Florida that was at that point particularly mad at the *Miami Herald* because they had just exposed corruption on the court and had had several judges removed, and we were on our way to the U.S. Supreme Court. It's fascinating because at the end of that argument in the Supreme Court it was obvious what the result would be. For the first time in my life I could sit there in front of that panel and say, Hey, we're going to win this one 9 to zip, and it's rare that you can do that.

Justice Blackman leaned forward to counsel for Tornillo, and said, "Counsel, I would like to ask a question," and then said, "No, I guess I wish to make a statement. For better or for worse in this country, we opted for a free press, not necessarily a fair press." I thought that was rather interesting, and I was certainly glad I was not counsel for the other side and had someone throw that statement at us.

But we must remember that early court opinions denied First Amendment protection to film, to movies. The court saw them to be "mere entertainment" and not part of the press. And as we saw this morning, states and cities began setting up boards of review of films and licensing films before they could be shown within their jurisdictions. Subsequently, our courts did change their views and granted First Amendment rights to film production. Today motion pictures are held to have the full protection of the First Amendment.

Radio allowed political leaders to have direct access to entire populations without the necessity of going through the information gatekeepers as did Washington or Lincoln in their day. We saw the rise of such leaders as Roosevelt, Churchill, Mussolini, and Hitler who utilized this fantastic medium to pass by the information gatekeepers and go directly to the public. In the United States with our unique concept of licensing of private individuals and companies in the broadcast field, we saw again the fear of those in power of letting full First Amendment rights flourish for these media. And with the adoption of the Radio Act of 1927 and the Federal Communications Act of 1934, we saw the creation of such things as the Fairness Doctrine, the Equal Opportunity provisions under section 315 of the Federal Communications Act, and, of course, the setting of standards of "decency" or "indecency," however you wish to view it, by federal regulators, even though denying that they're engaged in censorship.

On the print side we have the postal service, which has exercised the right of censorship for keeping certain materials out of the mails. And after World War II we saw the advent of television as a mass medium in this country which has become not only a medium of entertainment, but a primary medium of news and other information.

Now we move into a new revolution, evidenced by the computer, cable television, "wireless cable television," satellite communication, video cassettes, teletext, optical laser discs, all of which enormously increase the quantity and diversity of information flows. Ironically enough, with all this increased ability to transmit information, we find a significant decline in the ability of Americans to make effective use of these information sources. The U.S. Department of Education has estimated there are more than 27 million adult functional illiterates in this country. It's been estimated that problems associated with functional illiteracy cost over $224 billion a year in welfare payments, crime, incompetent job performance, lost tax revenues, and remedial education. The cost in terms of human misery cannot be estimated. So, truly, I think illiteracy is probably the cruelest censor of them all, and I would like some comment from our panelists as to how they're going to deal with this and the new technologies. We have computer illiterates in the country as we know, but what about the basic illiterates? Well I remain firmly convinced that just as we have in the past, sometimes much too slowly, we will succeed in applying First Amendment principles to complex and changing conditions to new technologies. We can and will do so. Not as rapidly as some of you might hope, and certainly not without difficulty and controversy, but the basic concept of First Amendment rights should be applied whenever and wherever possible to all forms of communication.

Someone mentioned this morning, I guess it was Dan Brenner, that the people who undertook to make these battles were often not exactly the kinds of persons that you'd like to take home to dinner, and I think one of the best quotes I've read on that in recent times comes from John D. Stevens who is head of the Department of Communications at the University of Michigan, in a wonderful book called *Shaping the First Amendment*. He described some of those people as follows:

Men and women who have been at the center of important free expression battles are for the most part a scruffy lot. If you do not long to take these people home for dinner, at least thank them for their fanaticism and their tenacity. Most of us shrink and shirk from testing values and laws. They did not.

And if you look at history, *Near* v. *Minnesota*, which Craig Smith has on his list—we didn't really get the first test of prior restraint and the concept of the First Amendment in this country until 1931, in that case of *Near* v. *Minnesota*. Jan Near was a virulent anti-Semite, a bigot, the kind of person that none of you would really like to have at your home for dinner, and yet the press in the country, and particularly Colonel Robert McCormick of Chicago, financed his fight to the Supreme Court. Even though Near was fighting everything that McCormick stood for, McCormick decided this man had a right to free speech and financed his fight to the Supreme Court.

One other favorite quote of mine concerning the First Amendment is in the form of a letter that author Kurt Vonnegut wrote to Judge John Newman, of the Second Circuit Court of Appeals, and I think this provides what may be the best description of that illusive yet essential quality of the First Amendment. And let's keep this in mind as we're trying to apply it to the new technologies. Vonnegut wrote, "The First Amendment reads more like a dream than a law, and no other country, so far as I know, has been crazy enough to include such a dream among its fundamental legal documents. I defend it because it has been so successful for two centuries in preserving our freedom and increasing our vitality, knowing all arguments in support of it are certain to sound absurd." So at this point, let's see how far we can go in coming up with these absurd arguments to apply them to the new technologies.

JOHN REDPATH, JR.

I think perhaps the first thing I should do is clarify the business of Home Box Office. We are not a cable company, we are a programmer. We are concerned about the health of the cable industry and we like to think the cable operators are our friends. They're the largest distributors of our products; they're our biggest customers. But Home Box Office is a programmer that distributes not only via cable but via Multipoint Distribution Service,

Multichannel Multipoint Distribution Service, and Satellite Master Antenna Television and Satellite. We are, in some respects, more of a pure First Amendment speaker than many other representatives that you'll see here today. We are not, fortunately, subject to a multitude of regulations that the cable industry or the broadcasting industry is subjected to. Many of us would argue that that's one of the reasons we have been fairly successful, and that it was only when some of the regulatory obstacles placed in our way by the FCC were removed by the courts that the Home Box Office was able to flourish and develop programming and develop the satellite television industry. The cable industry had the incentive and the resources to expand into those areas of the country where the additional programming that they could bring to the viewer would give them viable business.

I would like to talk briefly just about one narrow aspect of the First Amendment. I think the topic of the First Amendment and new technology is too broad to cover in a day, much less in an hour-and-a-half panel. What I would like to discuss is the indecency regulation as it is espoused by some state and municipal governments today and, unfortunately, in some of its aspects, even by the FCC. First, I think it's interesting to note that every time the question of indecency regulation has been put before the voters, and it's been put to a vote in towns in Texas and here in California, and most interestingly, in a statewide referendum in Utah, the proponents of banning and regulating "indecent programming" have lost. The label "indecent programming" is one that I find objectionable, but, unfortunately, it seems to have gained currency—that's one victory for the regulators. That label already puts those of us who like to express ourselves at a disadvantage. We have found that this sort of regulation is not popular with the people but there are elements in society that are powerful enough and vocal enough that they're able to persuade politicians, whether weak-willed or not I cannot say, but they've managed to persuade politicians to pass laws, or threaten to pass laws and ordinances that would regulate indecency. And what we're really talking about here when we speak of indecency is nudity. This seems to be the main thrust of these regulations.

In the courts, we and other members of the cable industry have had success, having won every single case that we have been involved in. The first of these arose in 1982, a case entitled *HBO v. Wilkinson*. The state of Utah had passed a statute that provided for criminal punishment to any person who knowingly distributes any pornographic or indecent material to subscribers. Let me say at this point that we at Home Box Office are not objecting, have never objected to the obscenity laws in this country. It is the laws that would prevent us from showing a movie like "Kramer v. Kramer" that cause us the most problems, and it is clear that these sorts of indecency regulations would do exactly that.

In any event, in 1982 the state of Utah passed this statute that we had attacked and the district court in Utah had no problem throwing out that law as vague and overbroad. The state, as you would expect, attempted to justify this regulation on the grounds that they were seeking to protect children in the state from being exposed to this sort of programming. The court, in its opinion, unfortunately did not deal with the *Pacifica* case, the Supreme Court case that permits the FCC to take action against Pacifica Broadcasting, which action happened to be placing a letter in the files of Pacifica. In that case a radio station, WBAI in New York, broadcast the well-known George Carlin comedy routine, "The Seven Dirty Words" or "The Seven Filthy Words." That broadcast had been heard by a man and his son driving in a car around 2:00 p.m. in the afternoon. They complained to the FCC and as I said, the FCC had put a letter in the file of the offending broadcast licensee. The Supreme Court affirmed on grounds that broadcasting was pervasive, which seems to mean that it comes into a person's home uninvited. There is some question, of course, about the uninvited nature of radio and television broadcasting, but the court seemed to feel that the pervasiveness, perhaps the free availability of these signals allowed the FCC to adopt a sort of nuisance rationale, and as I said, to place this letter in the licensee's file. The court also felt that broadcasting was uniquely accessible to children and that this gave the FCC another ground to restrict this type of programming.

But, back to Utah: Roy City in that state passed an ordinance that would have allowed the city to suspend the license of the local cable company if they broadcast indecent programming. Once again the district court, same judge, threw this out, this time examining *Pacifica* and finding significant differences between broadcasting and cable. I think I won't go into those at great depth but suffice it to say that it was the element of choice in the selection of a program on Home Box Office that the court saw as a significant difference.

The indecency movement next went to Miami where the mayor, after a visit to New York and a viewing of the public access channels there, returned home and got a similar ordinance passed that allowed the city to suspend or fine the local cable operator. As an interesting aside, the cable operator was required by its franchise to defend all elements and all parts of that franchise so that when we and a disgruntled consumer sued to have the ordinance declared unconstitutional, the cable operator was forced to join in on the side of the city. The cable operator sought to withdraw and a member of the city attorney's office was heard to tell the cable operator that he would get him for having made this motion to withdraw. So I think we have to keep in mind that the pressures that can be brought on cable operators and other programmers by regulators are often not so subtle and do not necessarily have to be legal pressures.

In any event, in *Cruse* v. *Ferre* the ordinance was overturned again on the grounds that it was over-broad and vague and that the right to regulate indecent programming on cable was not permissible because of the First

Amendment. The 11th Circuit affirmed the district court's decision on First Amendment and due process grounds. The ordinance had provided for complaints to be brought by the city manager and allowed the city manager to act as judge in those cases.

The final case in this litany of indecency regulation was *Community Television* v. *Utah*. Once again an indecency regulation was thrown out by the district court, thrown out by the 10th Circuit. The Supreme Court in a 7 to 2 decision affirmed the 10th Circuit opinion, Justice O'Connor and Chief Justice Rehnquist, voting in favor of putting this on oral argument. To quickly close, it seems to me that the course of this regulation indicates a couple of things about the First Amendment and new technology. One, it's not the technology that is going to determine an industry's or a business's or a technology's First Amendment treatment, it is the characteristics of that technology. And we find that the element of choice in cable and premium programming is what differentiates it from the broadcasting medium, not the wire as opposed to the airwaves. And secondly, in looking at the example of cable, it has been helpful that these First Amendment decisions come after cable had first begun and had a chance to develop. I think if many of these First Amendment questions had been brought by the cable industry in the 1950s or the 1960s or early 1970s, the answers would be very different from what they are today.

LEE BURDICK

For the last year, I have been directing a program for the Media Institute called The First Amendment Center for the New Media. It speaks to the topic of the new technologies and how the First Amendment applies to them. One point that should be noted at the outset is that the First Amendment is not an ideological issue. No matter which side of the political spectrum you are on, you have to believe in the freedom of people to communicate ideas.

Historically, we as a nation have come to believe that truth will ultimately prevail only where you have competition in the marketplace of ideas. And it is with this in mind that the Media Institute began our efforts to secure full First Amendment rights for the new media technologies. We have become involved with many new technologies that we see threatened by an increasing trend in the courts, the regulatory agencies, and the Congress to regulate without regard to First Amendment rights. It is because of this work that we've come to realize a couple of things. First, in this day and age the marketplace of ideas is, in fact, an economic marketplace. The second point is that because it is an economic marketplace too many companies and too many industries are willing to compromise and negotiate away their First Amendment rights in order to protect their economic interests. This fact has incredible ramifications for the public as well as new media speakers who may develop in the future. The final point that I would like to make today is that we cannot allow this to happen. We cannot leave the First Amendment in the hands of those trying to protect economic interests, because it means that the First Amendment may not survive the third century. Such a development would have a detrimental impact on popular democracy in our nation as it has developed over the last two centuries.

So let me go back to the first point, which is that the marketplace of ideas is, in fact, an economic one. If you look at the major business conglomerates that have come to control a substantial number of newspaper and broadcast and cable interests, you cannot help but notice the incredible values that are being placed upon them. Henry Geller cites some examples of the prices that are currently being paid for broadcast properties, and that most of this money is going not for the assets of the broadcast entity, but for the purchase of a license; and that we, the public, should ultimately be the beneficiaries of such a purchase, and not the individual who possesses the free license. Henry may be correct in that regard, but the phenomenon is certainly not limited to the broadcast industry.

If you want to look at Capital Cities ABC, which owns both broadcast and a substantial amount of newspaper entities, their revenues last year were $1.2 billion. The Rupert Murdock communications empire, both in this country and abroad, brought in $2.5 billion in revenues. We should not look at these companies in terms of revenues. We should be looking at assets and at what the companies would sell for if they were to sell. But the fact that these communications corporations bring in such large annual revenues means they are going to demand an incredible price.

The August 31, 1987 issue of *Broadcasting Magazine* did a comparative valuation between the broadcasting industry and the cable industry. And believe it or not, they came to the conclusion that the cable industry is by far more highly valued than the broadcasting industry. Cable plant and sales value totals $67 billion, while the broadcast industry as it exists today could only be valued at $38 billion, which is mind-boggling to me considering that cable has been around and allowed to develop freely such a relatively short time compared to the broadcasting industry. At the same time, when we begin talking about communication entities that are worth billions of dollars, you must conclude that it is an economic marketplace of ideas. So how does that apply or impact on the First Amendment and its protections? Problems arise when you have a business entity or an industry that has such an incredible economic interest to protect. After all, they are businessmen with bottom dollars to look at. All too often they are willing to compromise their First Amendment rights in order to protect their bottom dollar, to protect the value of their communications property. And this is true no matter which media you look at. Traditionally, we have believed that the true advocates of the First Amendment are the traditional newspapers. They fought for 200 years in order to secure strict First Amendment protection for themselves, and we expect them to continue. Yet, in another context, look at Judge Harold Green's application of the AT & T divestiture agreement, where the Bell Operating Companies (BOC) are now seeking to provide more than just common carrier service, but also electronic publishing and other information services. Their biggest competitor in that area, the organization that has given them the most flack, is the American Newspaper Publishers Association. ANPA has spent probably millions of dollars in legal fees developing this "Diversity Principle" of the First Amendment, which says that, if you have a company that through its anticompetitive behavior will drive speakers from the marketplace, then it is the court's obligation to prevent that company from entering the marketplace in order to promote diversity.

It was a similar point that Henry brought up in the context of broadcast and cable: where there is a limited numler of speakers who can access that marketplace, you have an obligation as a government entity to promote "diversification." Whatever the label, we are talking about taking the First Amendment, which says "Congress shall make no law abridging the freedom of speech and of the press," and turning it on its head to give government some justification to intrude into content and who may enter the publishing business. But my point is that it is the traditional press publisher who is now trying to use the First Amendment as a justification for government regulation of other media speakers.

In the broadcast area, there is a situation where the broadcasters this year were presented with an opportunity to fight for strict First Amendment protection by advocating repeal of the Fairness Doctrine. And yet, because there was before Congress another law that concerned license renewal, the broadcasters held off in their fight for repeal of the Fairness Doctrine for fear that there would be retribution in the enactment of legislation regarding license renewal. In other words, the broadcasters were more than willing to give up First Amendment protection that they could have won—and ultimately did, though it is still not dead—in favor of protecting the economic renewal interest in their broadcast property.

The cable industry won an incredible decision in the *Quincy* case, saying that it was unconstitutional under the First Amendment for the government to mandate that they carry the broadcast signals of competitors in their own market. Yet we see that the cable industry is quickly backing away from those First Amendment rights because they know that if the courts allow them strict First Amendment protection, those same First Amendment rights will invalidate their exclusive franchises. They don't want to lose exclusive franchising naturally, because of the economic impact it would have on their businesses.

Finally, we come to the telephone companies who, until a few days ago, were on the right side of the First Amendment in their battle to become electronic publishers. Now they are not talking about just being common carriers to provide for the speech of others, much as the post office does in facilitating exchange of others' mail. The telephone companies want to speak. They want to provide electronic yellow pages, electronic white pages, and on-line databases. They have yet to delineate any further ideas or speech that they would like to promote, but the idea is that they should be allowed the freedom—as we all should—to generate ideas and programming.

However, just the other day, *Communications Week* reported that even while certain Bell companies—namely, Pacific Telesis and Bell Atlantic—are fighting very hard to gain the First Amendment right to provide content, companies such as U.S. West are secretly negotiating with the American Newspaper Publishers Association in an effort to get ANPA to back off from their First Amendment position. In exchange, U.S. West is giving up its desire to provide certain kinds of content, so that it will acquire *some* ground in the information services area: What is troubling is that they are willing to forego their First Amendment right to speak in order to gain that ground.

That is a frightening but ever more frequent scenario, and it brings us to our ultimate conclusion, which is that we cannot leave the First Amendment in the hands of business entities to save for the rest of us. The onus is on us, the public, to guarantee that the First Amendment remains clean and pure, because it speaks to *our* right to get information and be able to make intelligent decisions, both about our government, about what products to consume, and about every aspect of how we conduct ourselves.

And if we allow these business entities to sully the First Amendment, it will have bad results for all of us. Ultimately it is up to you and me as individual communicators, as individual citizen voters, to be sensitive to the threats facing the First Amendment, and to be responsive to those threats.

EDWARD T. REILLY, JR.

When considering the future of freedom of the press in an electronic environment, I think it's useful to keep in mind the original intention of the founding fathers: Encouraging free access of expression by anyone who chooses to speak and free access to those speakers' ideas by anyone who is inclined to listen. It has taken us 200 years of legal regulatory and commercial development to establish a system that provides for a reasonable approximation of the practice of both of these freedoms—expression and listening.

New technologies have not inherited all of the legal immunities that were won for the old. As we move toward speech being conducted more and more via newer technologies, the right of citizens to speak without controls and to hear what they choose may be endangered. We must balance the practical need to organize technologically sophisticated delivery systems so that they bear the fruit of which they're capable, while ensuring that the essential advantages they provide are not denied to the general population.

In my own field, for example, the relationship between broadcasters, cable operators, and others who would wish to deliver video signals to homes via some "hard-wired" manner or via satellite transmission, is complicated and rapidly evolving. It pits the economic interests and varied capabilities of these different parties against each other. In this environment consider the goals for the video distribution system in this country. I believe they have been and should continue to be threefold and largely interrelated: promotion of competition, promotion of diversity, and maintenance of localism.

Competition will work toward improving the selection and production of entertainment and news, at least insofar as they appeal to the greatest number of people. Diversity helps produce a varied array of entertainment and news programming from which to choose. And localism, helping to offer an assurance that the power of the video press does not become too centralized, and that news and public affairs programming remains relevant to individual communities and that communities such as San Diego maintain their identity.

Here's a partial list of the regulatory issues that currently represent areas of controversy and will affect the nature and vitality and composition of the video industry. Must-carry regulations, compulsory licensing provisions, syndicated exclusivity, channel positioning, the future of the Fairness Doctrine, limitations on the networks' financial interest in programming production, spectrum allocation and the resolution of standards for advanced or high definition television, and the role of satellite-delivered programming. Each one of these issues, depending on how the regulatory environment evolves, can make a significant difference in the economic or creative vitality of the various points of interest involved.

As you might expect, I'm biased toward the maintenance of a strong locally oriented broadcasting environment. Not just because I'm part of it, but because I believe it has served our country well, particularly in the area of news commitment made by local television stations all across the country.

As the complex mix of regulations is *currently* structured, most local television stations recognize the significant obligation of local news. As a group, broadcasters devote the efforts of thousands of people and spend between $1.5 and $2 billion a year in that effort. I believe it's a good thing that the physical limitations of distribution kept us from having "national newspapers" for most of our history, thereby encouraging wider diversity of opinion. Similarly, I believe that having hundreds of news directors and producers independently deciding what is relevant in their community is a good thing for our country as we try to build consensus on the issues of the day and give many different points of view an opportunity to surface.

Satellite technology makes it possible for me to speak with you from the nation's capital tonight. It also makes it possible to add a new dimension of local editing of national and international news. It will allow the video press to continue with the tradition of a local press. In an environment in which most of our cities can support one or at most two newspapers' voices, it must be in our best interest to encourage the continued maintenance of three or more television voices that are viable in even the smaller cities of the United States. Television news, the principal source of news to over 50 percent of the people in the United States, is too important to allow weakening of this diversity.

As with many issues on the technological landscape, the regulation of cable operators and their relationship to local communities and broadcasters is very complex, pitting the First Amendment, the principles of capitalist competition and economic and technical realities against each other.

Cable adds a whole new improved dimension to television. We must look to continue to encourage even greater video competition and diversity, but maintain our commitment to localism. We must maintain an environment that provides the availability of free broadcast television to all of our citizens, wealthy or poor, particularly in the area of news. Cable operators must have First Amendment rights, but only insofar as they actively choose to participate as speakers. Like it or not, they have legal or at least de facto economic monopolies and, therefore, many of the characteristics of common carriers. A regulatory mix must be formed that protects their legitimate right to "speak" freely, but does not foster an economic environment which severely damages the financial ability of the broadcasting industry to provide "free" sports, entertainment, and news to the U.S. consumer. While nothing is truly free, advertising-supported television is a real bargain. The total industry costs the U.S. public about $20 billion a year, which is about $235 per year per TV household, passed along in the form of advertising allotments of consumer expenditures. That's about 65 cents per day or 10 cents per average hour of viewing. Advertising support of media—newspapers, magazines, radio, and television—provides for the expensive process of gathering and distributing news to mass audiences free or inexpensively. I believe we all prefer this method to either government funding or media so expensive that only the elite can afford to be informed.

Character-based information products are changing rapidly and will increasingly be stored and delivered through advanced technological means. Speakers' rights of access to these new technologies must be guaranteed as well as listeners' or readers' rights to access that information. The gatekeepers of new technology must not be given monopolistic control over the use of each new medium. We must still work to develop the distribution systems that will make these new technologies pay off. Present-day libraries, schools, bookstores, newsstands, printers, authors, editors, and publishers all need electronic updates or equivalents.

At the same time, we must recognize that television has become the medium of choice, rightly or wrongly, for the vast majority of citizens of our country. We must be sure that we use it not only to entertain, but to further the founding fathers' goals of providing for an informed, involved electorate.

I hope these issues raise some discussion. I'm sure they will on the part of those of you attending and some of the other speakers, and I'll be glad if we can pull this electronic telephone transfer together, to respond and benefit from the thinking that you've all given to these issues as well.

QUESTIONS AND ANSWERS

Moderator: We shall now give members of the audience an opportunity to ask questions of the speaker. First question, please.

I am *Martin Colby* and I am the General Manager of XETV Channel 6 here in San Diego. This morning we have been talking about the First Amendment as it relates essentially to domestic United States applications. But with the advancing technology that we are seeing growing on the horizon, satellite-delivered information, I would like to ask members of the panel their feelings or opinions of the application of the First Amendment to the eventual dissemination of information, or distribution of information, to the United States from outside the borders of the United States via satellite delivery from foreign countries, for example, or foreign sources. Is there a potential conflict arising with the First Amendment in this growing technology? And I address it to the panel.

Schmidt: I think there's definitely potential for conflict. If you look at the vote in the United Nations on transborder flows of information, the United States has been almost alone in calling for free flow of information. The rest of the world doesn't like our system, they don't want our commercials sailing across their borders, and there are all kinds of proposals for international control of signals across the way. It is going to be a tough call here because once you do that, if we are the only people calling for the free flow, it is going to be pretty tough to say, Well, hey, wait a minute. We are going to let everybody shoot into us, but we are going to sit there alone in that regard, because we have no access to theirs. I think that is where the conflict is going to come.

Question: Do you see the potential of inflow of information, for example, from the Soviet Union to the United States via satellite delivery?

Maines: Of course. And when you get into this afternoon's panel with Larry Scharff and the rest, when you get into this whole area of the satellites and what they are able to show today, you are going to get into some really interesting problems. I don't think there are going to be any secrets left in the world among other things, and everybody who wants to shoot their ideas in is sure going to have a chance to do so. You can read right now, as I understand it, a license plate number in the Kremlin parking lot. What the hell's left? Not that I want to buy a car there.

Geller: As a practical matter, satellite spills over in its footprint. In Europe they have satellite spillover from one country into the other, because countries are so small. Our signals dominate Canada because, again, so much of the Canadian population, for example, is within 100 miles of the border.

With regard to international broadcasting, we, of course, want open communication and no jamming. When you get to video, the problem is technically finding a way in because you can get reception, even with satellites, in a manner that will work and be compatible with that country—not run into interference.

The Soviet Union, for example, is a strong member of the International Telecommunications Union and would not interfere, because they don't want interference in their own, and working that out, the downlinks and so on, is not easy technically.

Redpath: I think the First Amendment has no application outside the borders of the United States. Most countries reject U.S. signals on a cultural basis. In Canada, for instance, Home Box Office is a fairly popular service, but we can't get any money out of that country, not because we don't have the rights at the moment, but because it is illegal for Canadian cable systems to carry Home Box Office. For years Canadians have viewed our signal for free, stolen it, in effect, just the way people did here in the United States, and the Canadian government really didn't do much about it. Now that we are able to extract some money from Canadians for viewing our programming, the government is getting upset. The recent trade treaty that was agreed to over the summer did nothing to provide us access into Canada. Mexico and the rest of the countries where our signal falls are often worse. They provide us no protection at all.

Schmidt: I think the more basic problem in what he questions, though, is not whether the First Amendment applies outside the United States. Obviously, it does not. They not only don't understand it, they don't approve of it and all that. But the question is, what happens when they start shooting in on direct broadcast satellite to your receiver, then what is your attitude going to be at HBO? Are you going to be saying, "Hey, the First Amendment applies to everybody including the aliens out there?"

Redpath: I can't imagine that we would attempt to stop those signals coming in.

Schmidt: You really can't?

Redpath: No.

Schmidt: Well they are certainly not one of those gutless wonders, Lee, that you talked about, albeit a rich gutless wonder. But I find that difficult to comprehend, that you would not want to take some type of protectionism on there. I think that is going to be a heck of a conflict with the First Amendment and U.S. business at that point.

Redpath: Well, I think the U.S. entertainment industry can go head to head with the foreign entertainment industry quite easily, and that we in Hollywood in the U.S. television industry don't have to worry about the signals coming in from Canada. We are already getting....

Schmidt: That is what General Motors said a few years back, too. We don't worry about those cars from....

Redpath: We are already getting all the talent out of Canada. They come to the United States to work.

Schmidt: I am glad you are secure in that feeling.

Burdick: If I could interrupt for just a moment, I would like to open up another international issue that I think might be of interest, and that is international access to U.S. information, particularly through electronic databases.

Recently, the Reagan administration passed rules and regulations under the auspices of the National Security Council giving the military, particularly the FBI and CIA, the authority to monitor U.S. electronic databases, electronic publishers if you will, to see if they are allowing access to foreign spies. One way they did this was sending out FBI representatives to Mead Data Central—which offers Lexis and Nexis—and to some of the other major database providers, who said, "Let us see your subscription list. Tell us what you're doing to monitor foreign access to this." They also went to libraries and they asked the librarians, "Do you know of any foreigners that are coming in and looking at your books and using your microfiche, or your electronic access to other libraries?"

Considering the history of the First Amendment, it was incredible that they could do this. It took a strong public reaction, a strong reaction from the electronic publishing Industry Information Association (IIA) to get that kind of regulation reversed. And even though they did get the presidential directive reversed, the ability to monitor national security and foreign access to electronic databases in this country still remains under the military side of government.

Moderator: Before we move on, let me check. Ed Reilly, are you with us?

Reilly: Yes, I am here.

Moderator: Would you like to comment on the question that was directed to the panel?

Reilly: Just in terms of the influence or impact it is going to give off, I think, outside the country more so than inside. I would not be so concerned about programs coming in, but obviously there is a significant difference, for example, if the Soviet Union has wide screen electronic technology to receive satellite programs through space. They must take on advanced electronic technology in order to keep their society competitive, and I suspect that is going to be good for us.

Moderator: Next question.

I am James Wilkin, Wilkin Broadcast Consultants, another panel question. Ed Reilly just used the words *video press*. My question is, is there such a thing as video press in context with the constitutional use of the word *press*? Would you define for me what is *press*?

Reilly: Yes, I think since video technology was not in existence when the founding fathers introduced the notion of the press, it was obviously not specifically included. But when one considers the role video transmission now plays in our society, it has all the characteristics that facilitate free exchange of ideas.

Schmidt: There is no doubt that television was not around and radio was not around, I was not even around, when they drafted the Bill of Rights.

Burdick: Reagan was.

Schmidt: Yes, Reagan was. They often start out saying, No, there is no First Amendment right, and then they come in and say, hey, wait a minute, this is beyond just entertainment. I think the Supreme Court once said what is one man's entertainment is another man's education. And this is the kind of thing that the courts have been flexible enough about, despite the doctrine of original intent. My grandmother used to say she refused to fly because she was scared to death of it. She said she was going to sit here on earth and watch television like God intended she should. But this is the kind of thing that the courts will evolve. I think it applies across the board. They don't differentiate between electronic and print media on this. It is the press, and I think Ed Reilly has come up with probably as good a definition as is possible. Dan Brenner said this morning that one of the problems is the definition of *press*. We get into that when you have things like shield laws and other definitions. It is very difficult to define *press* because a lonely pamphleteer is a member of the press just as much as your organization is, or the *Washington Post* or the *New York Times*.

Geller: I just want to point to the questions here; you noticed in the first one it says, How do variations and interpretation of the amendment affect its application to the press, broadcasting, cable? You shouldn't say that. Broadcasting clearly is the press. It is entitled to call for First Amendment values. So is cable.

Question: Then you can't go against the First Amendment if you interpret press that way correctly.

Geller: The difficulty is that each medium is regulated under the First Amendment in a different fashion. In broadcasting, they are entitled to core First Amendment values—by that I mean that the Supreme Court said government can't say that broadcasters can't present Democrats, or Republicans, or red-headed men. It would not survive for a second. You come under the same press shield laws, and similar acts. The problem comes under the Fairness Doctrine because of the public trustee notion. What I am saying is that you have the core First Amendment values. You are the press, you have to be.

Wilkin: I am also a destroyed broadcaster, because I was accused of violating the Fairness Doctrine on 22 counts, including that of personal conspiracy. It took four years to get an answer, and they gave the license back to the station quietly one night. And I asked them, why all the beef? And they said to me, the FCC, well we didn't find anything, did we? My response to that was, where do I go to get my reputation back?

Geller: I hear you and I tell you that it is a public trustee notion.

Wilkin: You abused it. You, personally, you abused the privilege. There was no First Amendment.

Moderator: We will allow the panelist to answer the question.

Wilkin: There is a court case there. You can see it.

Burdick: I would like to field that one for just a moment. The public trustee concept in broadcasting has been batted around for a long time. In fact at dinner last night, I was talking with Commissioner James Quello, and he said that if he could walk away from this conference with one thing, he would like to know how the public trustee concept should fit in relation to the First Amendment. How should it be molded in light of these tremendous freedoms guaranteed by the First Amendment?

My answer is this: Let the public decide what the public interest is. Let the public exercise (1) through their consumer decisions whether or not they want to turn on a station or turn off a station; and beyond that, (2) if they don't feel they are effective enough in exercising their consumer discretion, then let them organize. For instance, Henry mentioned on the first panel that there was a station in Mississippi that back in 1960 or 1961 lost its license because it presented racially slanted programming. It was only through the organization of the public reacting to that kind of behavior that got the license revoked, and that is exactly the kind of freedom, public freedom, to exercise their First Amendment rights that is going to bring about press responsibility.

Press responsibility cannot be legislated. It cannot be regulated. To the degree that government wants to police the airwaves to make sure that these public trustees do not interfere with each other's signals—to make a nice clean signal to your home TV or radio—let them do so, but limit it to that. Let the public decide what the value of those ideas are that come across. Let them decide how important fairness is to them and what fairness is.

Geller: The public got rid of that station by going to the government, and the government through the Court of Appeals got rid of it. Without the government it would still be operating as a racist station.

Burdick: Not true, not true at all. And I think this brings into context a very recent situation in Washington, D.C. Some of you may have read about it because it was quite highly publicized. We tend to think that, because the public can't seek a legislative fix against the traditional press (newspapers), they are held unaccountable. Well that is just not true. Nor would it be true for broadcasters if you eliminated this public trustee fairness.

The example I would like to give is this: The *Washington Post* started a new magazine at the beginning of last summer. The first two issues played up lead articles making blacks look bad. Both articles were very highly placed articles, and both of them looked at bad aspects of individual black members in the community. The black community responded by protesting. They claimed that by placing these two articles so prominently, the *Post* made them look bad and gave the appearance that the *Post* is racially slanted.

The black community couldn't go to the FCC or the Court of Appeals for a remedy. They didn't have a legislative fix available, and yet they fixed it by organizing and protesting in front of the *Washington Post*. They got what they wanted. The *Washington Post* said we are going to reevaluate our editorial policy. Beyond that, they got free local air time where *Washington Post* representatives went on the air and discussed the issues with black leaders in the community. And I suggest that it is exactly through that kind of public action that we are going to bring about fairness in the press, whether it is newspapers, broadcasting, or cable TV.

Geller: Let me ask you, then: Since there are no longer public trustees or you just like a newspaper, I take it you would be willing to auction the frequency?

Burdick: I'm for it, Henry. I'm for it.

Geller: We are all together. There is no disagreement on this panel at all.

Burdick: If we are talking about economic interests, let's call it as we see it, and let the public decide what those properties or those ideas are worth to them.

Geller: The broadcasters are not for it. They are the ones who don't want it and will take any. . . .

Burdick: Why is that, Henry? Because they are protecting their economic interests. That is my point. We can't leave the First Amendment to the protection of those looking to fulfill and promote their own economic interests.

Moderator: Next question.

Moreno: I am Ed Moreno and I am with KCET which, as you know, is part of the public television system, and it is considered also the weakest sister in the broadcasting system. Assuming that we were able to get rid of both the Fairness Doctrine and the public interest trustee concepts and that the spectrum fee became a reality, to what extent, then, would public telecommunications be deregulated and to what extent would both the public interest and the government interest prevail to maintain some kind of nongovernmental regulation?

Moderator: Directed to the panel or any member?

Moreno: Probably to the panel.

Geller: That is obviously something that I believe should happen. I think you would have to insulate public broadcasting from the government, which is passing the money on to public telecommunications, and there are ways to do that better than what we have today. But, as I said, once you do that and take the money either from an auction or spectrum usage fee, the broadcaster no longer has to operate then as a public trustee. I don't think you would notice a difference. There are very few WLBTs; that is the Mississippi station I referred to. For the most part, the networks dominate television, and if the FCC disappeared tomorrow, you would never know it. You would see the same thing. The FCC has no effect at all on entertainment programming and that is the bulk of what is presented. I think it is absurd to call the over 9,000 radio stations public trustees. They are out there in a very competitive market trying to find their niche, and usually playing music most of the time and then ripping and reading some news every five minutes on the hour to say the atom bomb hasn't fallen. You can continue to listen. I think that if you did this, if you deregulated, you would make sense out of the industry. You would have money then that would go to public broadcasting, which is motivated to do in-depth informational, to do children's programming, to do Shakespeare, to do programs for minorities. We would all be better off.

Burdick: I think your question was "to what extent should telecommunications be deregulated?" Clearly from the first panel we discovered that there are certain things about new kinds of communications that do need to be regulated. In broadcasting, we need to make sure that you don't have a cacophony of signals overrunning each other so that the public receives nothing but gibberish. In cable, you have a wire that traverses the public rights-of-way and the cities have a right to make sure that their streets aren't constantly in disrepair because new cable operators come in, dig up any street they wish, lay in their wire, and then cover the hole or not cover the hole. The cities have a thing to protect there.

So to the degree that you have a legitimate state interest to protect, then, yes, there should be some regulation to protect that interest. But when the state interest exceeds that minimal amount of regulation, when it gets into content-related things like access channels, equal time for political candidates and Fairness Doctrine of covering controversial subjects fairly, the regulations begin to traduce First Amendment values. So the long answer to your short question is that the media should be deregulated to the extent that we get government out of content, and regulate it only minimally to the degree necessary to protect the public interest in clean, undisrupted streets and nice, clean, quality signals through the airwaves.

Redpath: Would you allow the deregulation of public broadcasting, allow them to sell any commercials, for example, that kind of thing?

Burdick: I think public broadcasting is a unique entity; if the government is concerned with public access and providing for the public right to speak over the airwaves, then the government should do more things like public broadcasting, which is to establish conduits for public speech. Where the government has established public broadcasting, it should continue to have substantial control over that medium. But their control should be limited to the conduit that *they* provide, and not to private communications media.

Redpath: I guess I would be a little bit concerned about the government favoring one speaker over another. I have a lot of problems with the must carry rules, since the must carry rules make it more difficult for us to get our services to the public. And when the government gets in that business, I think we at Home Box Office are damaged by it and I think First Amendment concerns are raised.

Moderator: Ed Reilly, do you have a comment?

Reilly: I think the must-carry rules have to be taken in context of the overall regulatory environment. We have a history of cable operators signing people up on their capability to deliver a specific broadcast television signal and then turning around and saying, well, now we are not going to carry that station or we are going to move it to another less crowded channel. I think if one season we were not available on the cable, that might not be of concern to most carriers. But I think in context of the history in which broadcasting is advertised as part of the sign-up offering to say now we are not going to carry those changes anymore, that goes against television's First Amendment consideration, because many people will no longer be maintaining antennas to receive over the air TV signals.

Moderator: We have time for one, perhaps two more questions. I will ask the panelists at this point to please keep your responses very brief.

David Hanken, Department of Telecommunications, City of Los Angeles: John Redpath previously spoke about the court's activities with regard to indecency in terms of the new technologies. However, with regard to the old technologies, the FCC has recently spoken on indecency. There are three cases that came up before the FCC, and in those cases, the FCC essentially broadened their definition of decency. In fact, if you look at the Carlin case, which John Redpath had referred to before, the commission basically said you had to give some sort of notice, and the program had to occur after 10:00 in the evening. Well, within those cases, certainly one did occur after 10:00 in the evening with a notice. So essentially, the FCC has broadened their indecency definition, and I was wondering what the panel thinks about it, especially in light of the discussion going on here with government staying out of the business of free speech.

Geller: I think that the FCC decisions are terrible. They originally restricted the *Pacifica* decision just to the "seven dirty words" and indicated even these could be said at 10:00 P.M. or afterward. So that the FCC was promoting the idea that parents are available to supervise children at 10:00 P.M. and now it is adult time. The programming can then be heard, and even in the *Pacifica* decision, the Supreme Court, as John knows, did say that its decision was restricted just to that case. The court said that it was not talking about Elizabethan comedy. The commission, which says that it wants to afford full First Amendment rights and believes in the print model, did an extraordinary thing in saying that the FCC was no longer going to restrict itself just to the *Pacifica* facts. Broadcasters now can't even do this programming at 10:00 P.M.: it is barred whenever children are listening, and children are listening even at midnight; you get a significant number of children below 12 years of age at midnight. That is an amazing fact and staggers you, but the Nielsen shows that.

Beyond even that one, the commission went on and said that "The Jerker" program here in San Diego was obscene, and that is an obscene decision by the FCC in my opinion. That is a program that had very strong and offensive language in it, but it dealt with a serious topic, AIDS, and it had serious redeeming value. It did not appeal to prurient interests, and I think the FCC acted in a disgraceful fashion, giving in to the Moral Majority.

Schmidt: I agree with Henry. I think those were awful decisions. I think it highlights, though, one of the problems with government activities in this field. These decisions came out of an FCC that spoke quite proudly and bravely of its defense of the First Amendment, and then they turn around and do something like this. These, of course, were radio broadcasting stations and they did not attempt to extend that regulation to cable programming services or cable television systems.

Burdick: I agree with Henry and the previous speaker. The American Society of Newspaper Editors went on record as decrying this activity by the FCC on behalf of the electronic brethren, too. And I see Mr. Quello sitting back there who voted for it and smiling at us. Jim, I don't want you to be the censor anymore than I would be. Sorry about that.

Moderator: Concluding question?

Question: I will make it quick. We have a problem in the cable industry. It is a business problem having to do with access to tenants in multiple dwelling units (MDUs), and it involves, I think, a balancing of First Amendment rights of the cable industry, and perhaps First Amendment rights of the listener against the property rights of the landlord. And the courts have come down on the side of the property rights of the landlord. Cox here in San Diego just lost a case having to do with the First Amendment rights of the cable operator to get access to MDUs. I wonder how the panel feels about that, and putting it into the context of the topic of the panel looking towards the future, it gets more troubling. Henry, you have kind of glowingly talked this morning about the day soon to come when our friends in the telephone company will be able to replace their wires with broadband fiber. The telephone company has no problem getting access to MDUs. The newspaper has no problem delivering their papers in apartment buildings. What is going to happen when the telephone company now has the broadband fiber delivering the same services as the cable operators, but we are blocked at the door?

Moderator: Brief response now from each panelist.

Geller: I think that would be very bad. I would agree with you. I would hope that localities and states would allow access for just compensation under the *Loretto* case and that it is a pity not to have such access. The Cable Act seems to be ambiguous on that, and the rights of way provision has not been construed as broadly. Maybe it can be expanded. The telephone company is not coming soon with fiber. If I gave that impression, that ain't so. I won't live to see it fully but you will: you're younger.

Burdick: I hate to sound dispassionate, but I have a hard time feeling sorry for the cable operator who is worried about the ease with which he can suddenly, by dropping one line into a multiple dwelling unit, suddenly access say a dozen apartments, and what a great windfall that would be versus having to individually wire twelve different houses along a one-mile strip. What you are talking about here is the apartment manager's right or the individuals living in those apartments, their right to choose whether they want your service to come into their building or if they want to drop a satellite master antenna up on the roof and pull down their own signals. It is a matter of public choice, and they should be the ones allowed to make that choice. Sometimes that choice is made when an individual contracts with a landlord to move into a certain building.

Redpath: I think that is a matter for the local property owner to decide. I am really not in favor of a lot of the access laws that some localities have.

Schmidt: I think you have a heck of a tough problem making that a First Amendment issue.

Reilly: I would have gone to the residents rather than the property owners. If they were interested, they would be willing to go a long way to get it.

Moderator: This concludes the session. Many people believe the underlying assumption of the First Amendment is the widest possible dissemination of information from diverse and antagonistic sources. We only occasionally today had antagonistic sources, but we certainly had a very diverse and broad set of opinions on these topics. I would like to give a warm thank you to all of our panelists and to Ed Reilly who joined us on the telephone. Thank you very much for your views today.

4

Responsibilities and Rights of the Media

David Laventhol

There is no more important topic to us in the media business than the First Amendment; accessing its durability, flexibility, and survivability at a time of technological change is something we ought to be continually doing, and I think this is very, very worthwhile. Times Mirror does have interests across the media spectrum, and we distribute information in a variety of ways from print to broadcasting, notes to satellite services to compact disc (CD) recording. So the concerns of this conference are indeed well focused from our perspective.

I'm not sure that some of the people, though, whom we've been reporting about this year would share fully our concern for protecting our right to tell private stories about public people. In fact, I have no doubt that some recent events will renew focus appropriately on the responsibilities as well as the rights of the media. I'm going to divide my time here today between talking about responsibilities and rights.

In addressing this subject, I would hope that the context of our democratic free-for-alls are kept in perspective. I'm vice-chairman of the International Press Institute, which is a London-based international organization whose mission is to help journalists around the world when they're in trouble. And in that role, I am continually reminded of the unique climate in which the media exists in this country. Some headlines from the institute's recent newsletters emphasize the climate in most of the rest of the world. For example, this was last month's issue. EDITOR MURDERED IN CHILE. FOURTH

NEWSMAN CAPTURED IN LEBANON. DAILY FALLS FOR VICTIM AND IT WAS SHUT DOWN IN INDONESIA. BRITISH MEDIA GAGGED. All that seems far from home and from what we're talking about today. In a way it is but I think it's an important reminder of our uniqueness as a country. And that uniqueness has had its price at times when journalistic malpractice leads to abuse.

Several years ago *Time* ran a cover story entitled "Accusing the Press: What Are Its Sins?" In the piece, *Time* detailed what some other press critics described as crimes against the public including inaccuracy, intrusiveness, bias, and arrogance.

And certainly the Gary Hart case and now the Douglas Ginsburg case leave questions as to how far the media and society, in general, should dig into the private lives of public figures. One observer noted last weekend after Ginsburg's withdrawal, "We're going to have either saints or liars for public positions," and that's about it. The line between what people need to know and the right of privacy may have been breached and may need to be redefined.

Yet I'm one that happens to think that the *Miami Herald* was correct in reporting about Gary Hart's affairs, because what was involved was the character and integrity of the leading candidate for president. I was in charge of the program for the American Newspaper Publishers' Association Convention in New York last May and, in fact, had arranged for Hart to speak to our group. Timing being everything, it turned out that Hart's first public statement following the herald of revelations was to the newspaper publishers' group. He stood up before almost all the publishers in the country and didn't tell the truth. We knew it at the time and so did he, and shortly afterwards he decided not to run. He blamed the press but, of course, he had no one to blame but himself. The *Miami Herald* could be faulted for imperfections and the execution of that story but not, in my opinion, for its pursuit of the story, which was fueled by Hart's own boasts and bravado.

In the Ginsburg case, the media were only one player among many. They were more of a carrier than a creator of information, but their vast influence and power were reflected in the dazzling speed with which events were reported and amplified to top the national agenda. How many people knew who Douglas Ginsburg was before late October, let alone his biography or his smoking habits?

These issues of press responsibilities are troubling, but hardly new. Justice Brandeis could have been talking about today's media when he and a law partner wrote in 1890 that "the press is overstepping in every direction the obvious bounds of propriety and of decency. Gossip is no longer the resource of the idle and the vicious but has become a trade which is pursued with industry as well as effrontery." Those are legitimate concerns now as well as then.

That is why Times Mirror decided two years to launch an ongoing national study with the Gallup organization about public attitudes toward the media entitled, "The People and the Press."

The first finding of our study may well be the most important. Despite a lot of criticism, there is no credibility crisis for the nation's news media. If credibility is defined as believability, then credibility is, in fact, one of the media's strongest suits. In fact, over 80 percent of the respondents found the major national news organizations to be either believable or highly believable. Nearly nine of ten Americans expressed a favorable opinion concerning the nation's media.

On the other hand, our survey clearly identified perceptions of what *Time* called "sins of the press." For example, only 55 percent of those polled in a national cross-section believe that news organizations get the facts straight; 34 percent find news coverage to be often inaccurate; more than half think the press tries to cover up its mistakes; only 34 percent believe the media is willing to admit its mistakes.

There's a lesson there and it's relatively simple, when we err—whether it's trivial or significant—we should admit it and correct the record promptly.

As I mentioned, the Times Mirror Gallup survey is an ongoing national study, and some new findings will be officially released next week. There are some continuing lessons in the latest results. First, the U.S. public does not agree with me about coverage of the Gary Hart affair. Sixty-eight percent of those surveyed think that news organizations went too far in reporting about Hart and Donna Rice. The public has similar objections to the coverage of the other presidential candidates. Sixty-five percent believe the press went too far with the story reporting that Pat Robertson's first child was conceived out of wedlock. Thirty-six percent felt that way about the story about Joe Biden's plagiarism.

Ironically, while the public thinks the press went too far in these particular instances, at the same time the majority believes the media should almost always report certain stories about presidential candidates including, if it were true, that a candidate was homosexual; 55 percent thought that should be reported. If a candidate exaggerated his academic record, 64 percent thought it should be reported. If he exaggerated his military record, 68 percent thought it should be reported. If he didn't pay any federal income tax, 65 percent thought it should be reported. Only 41 percent believe a candidate's extramarital affair should be reported. Thirty-six percent think that an arrest during college for marijuana should be reported.

Asked an open-ended question about what they disliked about press coverage of the presidential campaign so far, 18 percent volunteered the press was too intrusive into candidate's personal lives. Our survey indicated the public is much more interested in the candidate's experience and stand on the issues than on personal character. Only 9 percent think it is the factor that should receive the most attention.

Yet stories about personal lives continue to captivate readers. Of five recent major news stories, the one that attracted the most widespread interest was the Jessica McClure story, the little girl in Texas who was rescued after falling into an abandoned well. Sixty-nine percent of the respondents, and this was a national sample, followed this very closely. Forty percent were interested in the stock market crash, and 38 percent in the U.S. Navy presence in the Persian Gulf. Only about 15 percent followed the presidential election coverage with the same degree of interest.

More disturbing were the findings in our original sample concerning the public's knowledge about press law and regulation. There is not only a lack of understanding, there's real misunderstanding. For example, 55 percent do not know that television stations are more closely regulated than newspapers.

Libel law is also widely misunderstood. Almost 75 percent of respondents did not know that libel laws are more protective of private citizens than public officials. Besides being unaware of this basic difference, the public doesn't seem to think there should be one. The poll asked this question: What if the facts in the story about a public official turned out to be false but the news organization believed the facts were true at the time of publication? Should the news organization have to pay damages or not? Sixty-seven percent of those surveyed felt the news organization should pay the damages for such an unintentional error. As you know, that is not the law.

While most of the U.S. public does not know that the First Amendment guarantees freedom of the press—in fact only three Americans in ten can tell us that the First Amendment is the part of the Constitution that mentions freedom of the press—the public does value the idea that government should stay out of the newsroom and that the press should play an energetic watchdog role. Sixty-seven percent believe that press criticism keeps leaders from doing things that should not be done.

All of this is a mass of statistics and there will be more as we continue our polling, and some of the findings seem contradictory. Overall, though, I think three main points emerge. First, there is strong public support for the media performing its watchdog role, and there's a strong believability in what appears in the press. Second, there is widespread concern about what are perceived as media excesses and fallabilities, particularly in terms of privacy issues. And third, there is an astounding lack of knowledge about some of the fundamental laws that govern press freedoms and that are so crucial to making our society work. To me, this means all of us, and not just the media, need to understand and communicate about our constitutional processes a lot better than we have. It also suggests the media's continuing need to focus on its responsibilities as well as on its rights.

I'd like to talk a little bit now about rights, the principal subject of this meeting. I certainly start from the absolutist position, and I guess this is where I'm not sure I see conflict among some of the media. Those few words, it seems to me, that begin "Congress shall pass no law" have withstood the test of time.

The protections of the First Amendment must be broad enough to encourage the publication of all manner of information and opinion, even if it is disagreeable, offensive, silly, or just plain stupid. And these protections are needed no matter whether the information is delivered by Pony Express or lap-top computers. These issues do play out differently in different media, and since Times Mirror is a multiple dimensional media company, these different perspectives are important to us.

Our first perspective is newspapers. In addition to the *Los Angeles Times*, we do publish several of the principal newspapers on the East Coast: *Newsday* in Long Island and New York, the *Sun* papers in Baltimore, the *Hartford Courant*, and several others.

Contrary to what Ted Turner and some others predicted a few years ago, newspapers are not dying. In fact, even in this era of vast technological change, we believe they're here to stay. We just recently made several commitments to back up our beliefs. Most notably, a $400 million investment in printing equipment and a new Los Angeles plant for *The Times*.

We do not expect delivery of the newspaper to be replaced by an electronic message delivered to your television or computer screen.

A few years ago we experimented in this field with one form of electronic delivery, Videotext, and we did find a technology that worked, but a consumer who preferred more traditional ways of receiving information. It was, in fact, a technology without a marketplace. There may be several reasons for the continuing vitality of print journalism, and you may have seen some of it when we were fiddling with this mike before. Newspapers are literate, comprehensive, portable, compact, and tangible. People want to read their news in a newspaper they can hold in their hands. They want to be able to move around the house with it, divide it up between family members. They want to cut out ads, cartoons, or articles and put them on a refrigerator door, and you can't clip an electronic message or take it with you to read while you're in the bathroom. So we believe newspapers are here to stay, and the rights of newspapers to publish must be strongly protected.

The Supreme Court's majority decision in the *Miami Herald* v. *Tornillo* suit in 1974 stated the case eloquently.

A newspaper is more than a passive receptacle or conduit for news comment and advertising. The choice of the material to go into a newspaper and the decisions made as to the limitations on the size and content of the paper, and treatment of public issues and public officials, whether fair or unfair, constitute the exercise of editorial control and judgment. It has yet to be demonstrated how government regulation of this crucial process can be exercised consistent with First Amendment guarantees of the free press as they have evolved to this day.

And that's certainly how we feel about newspapers and the First Amendment, and we think it has a durable future protecting the rights of newspapers to print.

The shape, however, of other media in the future is much less certain, and the free flow of information in those media, which this conference is focusing on, is certainly less secure. Times Mirror, as mentioned, has a major interest in this area. We own four television stations, have more than 900,000 basic cable subscribers, and operate several information-based professional publishing businesses.

The broadcasting and cable industries are now wrestling with the future of high-definition television, a new development that could revolutionize the media and require tremendous investment of capital in order to meet the demands of the technology. Network audience levels are down as options such as cable, VCRs, and satellite transmission abroad. About 47 percent of U.S. television households are now on cable, and we expect that number to increase to more than 60 percent by the turn of the century.

One of the most significant changes is the use of computerized processes to gather, store, and distribute information. For example, one of our subsidiaries, Matthew Bender, the legal publishing company, is investing significantly to develop ways to deliver up-to-date legal research and analysis via computer. Rather than using a form from a book, for example, lawyers will be able to pull one out of their computer memory bank and then edit it in their own word processing computer to fit their client's particular needs. As is being discussed at this conference, courts will face the issue of whether legal and constitutional protections will apply to information that is delivered by a new technology. We believe that traditional protection should apply, even if the medium is untraditional.

A New York judge recently faced that very question. An investor sued Dow Jones after he lost money on an investment in a Canadian company. The investor blamed the newspaper publisher because an article on the company did not explain that certain prices were in Canadian dollars, not U.S. dollars. There was a slight twist to this case, however. The investor did not read the information in the *Wall Street Journal*. He read it on his personal computer. He was a subscriber to the Dow Jones News Service on-line computer service.

The judge had to decide whether he should apply different legal rules to the new technology. He decided not to, and I'm now quoting from what he said. "If the substance of a transaction has not changed, new technology does not require a new legal rule merely because of its novelty," explained the judge. It was New York Civil Judge Louis R. Friedman. In his ruling he noted that the investor asserted that "this case is different from one involving a newspaper; however, he provides no reason for treating a person who reads data on a computer screen differently from one who reads it on paper. The potential devastating effect of a holding of liability on the publisher is no different. The potential harm to the free dissemination of news and ideas is the same." Dow Jones News Service, the judge concluded, "is one of the modern technologically, interesting, alternative ways the public may obtain up to the minute news. It is entitled to the same protection as more established means of news distribution."

The First Amendment issue is at center stage in broadcast television again this week as Congress renews efforts to write the Fairness Doctrine into law. Since the Fairness Doctrine was dropped by the FCC in August, it is interesting to note there has not been any surge in fairness complaints, according to the editors of *Broadcasting Magazine*, which is a Times Mirror publication now. There has been no change in the level of audience complaint, and in fact during this time there has not been one complaint serious enough to call a station before the FCC for further review.

This certainly has been true in our own television station. Fairness Doctrine or no, the stations are not operating any differently, and have maintained their philosophy of presenting both sides of the controversy. During a local election campaign on a bond issue in Saint Louis, one of the sides wrote to our station, KGB, and asked for free air time quoting the Fairness Doctrine. We granted the time in the same way we would have if the Fairness Doctrine were, in fact, still in existence. So we don't think that the end of the Fairness Doctrine will mean an end to fairness. It's demise may even portend a greater period of freedom to deal with controversial topics that have remained off the air in the past. The multiplicity of broadcast voices that now exist ought to have rendered this doctrine obsolete, and the proposal to reimpose it by legislation, and even impose monetary penalties for violations, should be rejected.

There are also broader ramifications for other media. As a *Broadcasting Magazine* editorial stated recently,

There can be no more important consideration for the proprietors of the printed press. The First Amendment of which they have grown accustomed is at risk everywhere these days. If ultimately the Fairness Doctrine becomes the law of the land for radio and television, it would be only a matter of time before it was extended.

On another front, as one of the country's largest cable operators, we are mindful of the tug-of-war between government regulators, cities, cable companies, and broadcasters concerning the legal rights for the cable industry. Is cable more like the print news media or more like broadcasting? In recent years there has developed a sliding scale of permissible regulations with newspapers and magazines representing the end of the spectrum with the least allowable regulation and the broadcast media the most heavily regulated. Thus, depending on whether cable is more like print or television, may dictate the level of allowable government intrusion into its affairs.

Cable television is somewhere between these extremes. Unlike newspapers, cable companies cannot operate completely independent of government because legal access to public rights of way are necessary to operate the business, either by stringing cable on public utility poles or laying it underneath public streets and sidewalks. In addition, in some communities, economic conditions may dictate that there is a natural monopoly in the cable business. In those areas, we believe it would be economic suicide to allow competition between cable companies, and the local residents would be the victims. However, recent federal court cases have seriously questioned the constitutionality of many regulations in cable. In Sacramento, for example, a federal court ruled that the cable television system was not a natural monopoly and competitors could not be restricted from entering the local market. And Santa Cruz's policy of awarding only one cable television franchise has also been declared unconstitutional. These cases have seriously confused the legal framework within which the government and cable companies operate. However, we continue to believe that under the First Amendment cable television may be subject to some level of noncontent regulation. At the same time, the government must continue to avoid any regulation of the content of information that is provided on cable channels.

From cable to broadcast to newspapers to database publishing, we believe that the free flow of information should not be impeded. There are some complex legal and technological issues involved, and responsibility must be the handmaiden of rights. But in the end, we would cite the powerful words of Judge Learned Hand to be applied as broadly as possible. "The First Amendment," he said, "presupposes that right conclusions are more likely to be gathered out of a multitude of tongues than through any kind of authoritative selection. To many this is, and always will be, folly; but we have staked our all upon it."

5

The First Amendment—National Security

J. Laurent Scharff and Jack E. Thomas

J. LAURENT SCHARFF

The last three decades have witnessed a virtual revolution in the capabilities of the remote-sensing satellite. The first such satellites—weather satellites launched by NASA in the early 1960s—had a resolution of only one kilometer, that is, the only objects visible in the imagery were 1-kilometer in size or larger. By the early 1970s, when NASA launched the first in a series of Landsat satellites, resolution had improved to 80 meters. The only fully functional Landsat satellite still in orbit today, the Landsat V, has a resolution of 30 meters. The highest-resolution Western commercial satellite now in order is the French Spot 1, which has a resolution of 10 meters. It is generally recognized that commercial satellites could be built today with a resolution as good as one to five meters. As a point of comparison, the remote-sensing satellites operated by the U.S. Intelligence community are reputed to have a resolution level of several inches.

Beginning with the launch of Spot 1 (Satellite pour observation de la terre) in February, 1986, the world has witnessed the beginnings of a proliferation of remote-sensing satellites, commercial satellites. The French have plans to launch a follow-on Spot satellite. The Japanese have launched an ocean remote-sensing satellite and plan to launch spacecraft with better

---

Robert J. Aamoth also contributed to preparing this presentation.
Used by permission of the Radio-Television News Directors Association, Inc.

resolution in the next few years. The Canadians are planning to launch a so-called "radarsat" (using radar rather than optics to record imagery) with a resolution level possibly better than 10 meters and a capability to "see" through clouds and at night. Even the USSR has gotten into the commercial remote-sensing business. The foreign trade associations' Soyuz Karta intends to sell remote-sensing imagery with a resolution as good as five or six meters and it is willing to sell to the world community, including the U.S. government, the press and the general public.

The United States, however, is mired in a debate over whether to remain a vigorous participant in the industry. Congress laid the groundwork for such involvement when it adopted the Land Remote-Sensing Commercialization Act of 1984 (Landsat Act). The primary purpose of the act was to facilitate the transfer of the Landsat program into private hands. That transfer was successfully accomplished in September, 1985, when EOSAT took the reins of Landsat. It has not yet been decided, however, whether or in what amount EOSAT will receive federal funds to continue the Landsat program. Because EOSAT claims those funds are essential for the survival of Landsat, the participation of the United States and the remote-sensing industry is on hold until that funding issue is resolved.

Title IV of the Landsat Act provides that *any* private organization may build, launch, and operate a commercial remote-sensing system upon obtaining a license from the Secretary of Commerce. It is Title IV that has sparked the debate between the press and government officials over the scope of the media's right to engage in remote-sensing journalism when considerations of national security are alleged to be present.

The watershed in the use of remote-sensing imagery by the press was the Chernobyl nuclear reactor accident in the USSR in April 1986. Chernobyl was the first time that all the major networks, the newspapers, used remote-sensing imagery at the same time to report a major breaking news story. Indeed, remote-sensing imagery from the Landsat V and Spot 1 satellites proved to be virtually the only independent information available to the Western world on a disaster with potentially global consequences. It is no understatement to say that Chernobyl first opened the eyes of the press to the unique contribution that remote-sensing imagery can make to the news business.

Apart from Chernobyl, remote-sensing imagery has been used over the past two years in news stories on a variety of subjects, notably in the Persian Gulf. The news media have used more remote-sensing imagery in news stories over the past two years than over the previous ten years combined. The principal reason behind this phenomenon has been the 10-meter imagery produced by the Spot 1 satellite. The only imagery available prior to that was Landsat V's 30-meter imagery, which generally did not provide the detailed information or the type of recognizable scenes needed by the news media.

The new-found usefulness of imagery to the press has led current vendors of remote-sensing imagery to explore new ways to serve the media market. For example, EOSAT recently announced that it would market what it calls STAR sensor specifically for news gathering purposes. STAR would be a high-resolution (5-meter) sensor placed on EOSAT's next generation of Landsat spacecraft planned for launch in the early 1990s. EOSAT wants news organizations to "subscribe" to this service, not just buy single images from it. EOSAT would also be willing to contract with a consortium to handle sales to the media members. There has been talk of the possibility of a news organization or a joint venture of organizations launching its own remote-sensing system dedicated to news gathering—a so-called mediasat. The principal attribute of a mediasat, other than its ownership and control, is likely to be high resolution on the order of three to five meters. Some individuals in the industry believe that a leap in resolution quality from Spot l's ten meters to a mediasat's three to five meters would be the catalyst for routine integration of remote-sensing imagery into the day-to-day business of gathering and reporting the news.

A legal prerequisite for launching EOSAT's STAR sensor or a mediasat would be a license from the Secretary of Commerce under the Landsat Act. While Title IV authorizes the Secretary to grant such a license, it also empowers the secretary of defense to impose restrictions. In particular, the Secretary is given virtually unbridled discretion to take a number of actions ranging from denying a license application to conditioning a license in the names of "national security" and "international obligations." The act nowhere defines those terms nor does it specify the *standards* that the Secretary must use when determining whether considerations of national security of international obligations rise to the level necessary under the First Amendment to justify imposing restrictions on the press.

Many in the press believe that the act violates the First Amendment in at least two ways. First, it is unconstitutional under the "void for vagueness" doctrine by failing to spell out with "narrow specificity" the situations in which restrictions will be imposed on the press and other users. Second, the statute authorizes the *secretary* to impose prior restraints and content-based restrictions on the press, in other words, to censor the press. The Supreme Court has held that such restrictions may be imposed only when the government proves by hard evidence, *in court*, that each restriction is necessary to prevent a direct, immediate and serious threat to the national security. The media are concerned that nothing in the Landsat Act specifically requires that standard to be applied.

A number of organizations, spearheaded by the Radio-Television News Directors Association, expressed these concerns to the National Oceanic and Atmospheric Administration after it issued proposed rules to implement the Landsat Act. NOAA's final rules, issued this past July, only heightened the media's concerns. While recognizing that the news media do have a

First Amendment right to engage in remote-sensing journalism, NOAA made no attempt to specify the standards that would be used to determine whether proposed restrictions on remote-sensing licensees, for reasons of national security and international obligations, are justified under applicable First Amendment criteria.

The media also are extremely concerned about NOAA's decision to defer entirely to the Department of Defense and the Department of State on these matters. That position raises even more questions as to whether the media's First Amendment rights will be fully protected by the licensing process. Perhaps most alarming—NOAA expressly reserved the right to seize any material, presumably including remote-sensing imagery and possibly data processing equipment in newsrooms, which the government believes is likely to be used in violation of the Landsat Act, its rules, or its conditions in a license. Under the language of the rule for seizure of what could be used unlawfully, an entire television station, newspaper, or magazine arguably might be subject to seizure. These broad provisions could result in unnecessary sacrifice of First Amendment freedoms in the name of "national security."

In fact, there is no inherent conflict between national security and the media's First Amendment right to engage in high-resolution remote sensing. The press regularly cooperates with government officials to prevent harm from public disclosure of information truly threatening national security. There is every reason to believe that remote-sensing journalism will be practiced as responsibly as conventional journalism has been for decades, and that in most cases, the media and the government will come to an agreement.

Even in situations where the media and the government cannot agree on the appropriateness of a restriction, the government has adequate recourse, short of outright censorship by the Executive Branch. The government will know in exact detail the orbital path of every commercial remote-sensing system under the Landsat Act's licensing scheme. That knowledge should give the government sufficient time to seek a court injunction against the press before the satellite is in a position to "see" the allegedly sensitive occurrence. If the government's case is justified and it is able to meet the constitutional standard for imposing a prior restraint, the national security interest at stake would be adequately protected by court order. NOAA's regulations, to the contrary, permit the government to restrain and seize first—and hold a hearing after.

On the plus side of national security, a privately funded high-resolution system would furnish the government an additional source of remote-sensing data. Whether it is used as a primary source of information not obtained through other means, or simply as a backstop to the government's own remote-sensing efforts, a mediasat or EOSAT STAR sensor could play a potentially valuable role in protecting the national security of the United

States. Finally, the justification for imposing restrictions on U.S. remote-sensing licensees erodes with each remote-sensing satellite launched by *foreign* countries. It is broadly known that, in 1978, President Carter issued Presidential Directive 37, which specified ten meters as the resolution level which civilian systems were not to exceed. The ten-meter barrier has already been breached by Soyuz Karta, the Russian trade association marketing five-to-six-meter imagery. Other foreign systems with similar resolution levels are on the drawing boards, and it is simply a matter of time before the ten-meter barrier is an historical relic. The United States cannot stop or even control advances in remote-sensing technology around the world. The greatest danger is that our government will relegate the nation's private interests, like those of EOSAT, to a permanent back seat in this emerging worldwide industry, in the pursuit of ephemeral protection of undefined "national security" interests.

The time has come for Defense, State, and Commerce Department officials to sit down for discussions with representatives of the news media and other existing and potential earth imagers and users of this imagery.

This dialogue could lead to proposals for Congress to amend the licensing provisions of the Landsat Act so as to encourage the private development of higher-resolution remote-sensing satellites. There is good reason to believe that this could be done in a manner that would protect the real needs of national security while ensuring maximization of public information about the surface of the earth and a renewed leadership role for U.S. interest in space.

JACK E. THOMAS

The lifeblood of a conference like this depends on the discussion that is stimulated, and from the makeup of this audience I sense that I'm that guy from the other side who is supposed to stimulate comments. I'm listed on the program as a consultant. I'm not here as an official spokesman who will tell you exactly what some future secretary of defense will do, but, as a consultant, I'll tell you what I think he will do. And after thirty years in uniform and eighteen years as a consultant handling matters related to the national security, I think I have some understanding as to what's involved, and I present the next few minutes from that standpoint.

Is there a national security problem with what's up in space now, imaging? No. None of these systems has the kind of near-real-time reporting or the high resolution that would create national security problems, particularly in time sensitive situations. But the technology is available to anyone who wants to pay what is now a high price, and the price is going down. Mr. Scharff mentioned that EOSAT hopes to launch in 1994 a 5-meter resolution satellite, provided that the media is prepared to pay for it, at a cost of $50–$100 million. It's a put up or stop talking sort of proposition, it strikes me, as of right now. The media have been talking for several years. They want a mediasat. Okay. You want to pay for it, here is a specific proposal. There was no evidence I can find that when the 1984 Commercialization Act was being discussed, anyone even thought about a mediasat. But there are eight separate places in that law that say any satellite system will be operated in support of the national security, and the law says that the secretary of defense shall determine—now, that's the operative word—shall determine when a system is or is not operating in support of the national security. And as Mr. Scharff mentioned, penalties can range as high as denial, or termination of the license.

Once representatives of the media became interested in the possibility of a mediasat, they sought to have the Department of Defense put in the rules that will implement the 1984 act, some specifics as to what support for the national security means, what national security concepts should be applied. Media representatives did not give any definition of what they thought the national security involved, but they complained about the lack of specificity in the proposed rules. The Defense Department from the beginning opposed any inclusion of specifics that went beyond the wording of the 1984 act on grounds that the future is so uncertain the hands of the secretary of defense should not be tied.

So what are the national security interests that would apply? I think everyone in this room could define national security to his or her satisfaction. Lawyers of the media are undoubtedly going to have a different view from the government's when push comes to shove. But the basic argument to date is, as Mr. Scharff pointed out, whether the rules are unconstitutionally vague. Government lawyers don't consider they are but in view of the litigious society in which we live, the first time any attempt is made to impose any kind of restriction, I'm sure we'll go right to court. And one of the factors that will have to be considered is, what are the national security interests that have to be protected?

Let me give you an official definition; this is the one that the Joint Chiefs of Staff use:

National security is a collective term encompassing both national defense and foreign relations of the United States; specifically, the condition provided by a military or defense advantage over any foreign nation or group of nations, a favorable foreign relations position, or a defense posture capable of successfully resisting hostile or destructive action from within or without, overt or covert.

I don't think that provides very good guidance for the kind of situation that we would have when a mediasat is up above us.

Suppose a mediasat were denied access to imagery of preparations to launch a U.S. effort to rescue 200 Americans who are held hostage in country X. Is the saving of those hostages, whose deaths would probably result from premature disclosure of the imagery, is that in the national security interest? Or is the national security involved only when the actual survival of the country is at stake? If the criteria are going to be as strict as all that, could you have justified denying access to imagery of the preparations for the landing at Grenada? Because that certainly was not something in which the immediate survival of the United States was involved. We never have had a case in which action taken to avoid the direct and virtually immediate death of Americans has gone to court as a First Amendment case, and because we live in a dangerous world that's fraught with certain uncertainties, the Department of Defense considers that the rules under which commercial systems will operate in the future need to allow some flexibility. That is essentially why the rules as promulgated by the Department of Commerce make no attempt to specify what the national security concerns are. They will depend on the manner in which the situation develops.

If a commercially operated, high-resolution imaging system with a near-real-time reporting capability actually is proposed for licensing, the Defense Department will have to be prepared to react promptly. If the application has all the data that the law calls for and the rules call for, I personally have no doubt whatever that the application will be accepted. The problems will arise, if there are ever going to be problems, after the imaging system is in operation, because then the action/reaction times would have to be very fast. If there are going to be problems, I believe they will relate to extremely time sensitive situations in which premature disclosure of imagery would put the lives of Americans directly and immediately at stake. The Department of Defense has to be in a position, in my view, to deny imaging access in situations like this.

Mr. Scharff mentioned that a 10-meter resolution limit is now a matter of government policy.[1] I think that for purposes of looking at the media's problem we should keep in mind that the unclassified national space policy merely says this: "Civil earth imaging from space will be permitted under controls when the requirements are justified and assessed in relation to civil benefits to the national security and foreign policy. These controls will be periodically reviewed to determine if the constraints should be revised."

Nothing has come along yet to require an examination of those constraints. No one has applied for a license under the existing rules. Policy decisions are made to fit situations as they exist. If a responsible party applies for a mediasat, I have no doubt in my mind but what any policy on resolution constraints would be reviewed, and I think we would get a decision that fits what's going on in the world. Certainly, one of the factors to be considered when an application is made is what resolution is available from foreign-operated systems. But you should keep in mind that all foreign-operated systems in existence today are government owned and the systems coming along will be government owned. Government-to-government negotiations certainly could be attempted to impose some kind of control if such was deemed necessary.

Any resolution limitations that exist today could be changed in short order in response to an application. I think we should keep in mind one of the statements that is in the present [Department of Defense] rules, and I quote:

> To the extent there is a tension between the policy of promoting the commercial use of remote sensing systems and the policies of promoting national security interests, as determined by the Secretary of Defense or international obligations as determined by the Secretary of State, the Secretary of Commerce may, in his or her discretion, undertake reasonable efforts to satisfactorily resolve the matter in favor of commercialization.

Now that's part of the rules that became effective in August. It was not in any of the earlier drafts. I saw it for the first time when the rules were finally printed. But I think it goes a considerable way toward meeting some of the concerns of the media, even though it's not in the kind of words that Mr. Scharff and his cohorts were proposing earlier.

When the media get beyond the debating stage and the talking stage and actually formulate a specific proposal for a mediasat, they will have the kind of resolution that they want and feel they can afford. I personally see no reason for them to have concern as to whether they'll get the license that they want with the resolution that they're asking for. But that situation hasn't arisen yet.

I mentioned earlier that as of this date we don't have any specific concerns about national security with respect to the available imagery. But I also mentioned that time can change once we get really high resolution, near-real-time reporting imaging systems in space. Up to now I think we've had probably more heat than enlightenment in a lot of the discussions I've had, not with Mr. Scharff personally, but with members of his profession.

The basic position presented to me by the media is "trust us. We don't trust you because you may be capricious, but trust us, we'll do what's right." And then I read a news columnist who quotes a correspondent for a U.S. national television network as declaring that he felt so free in his view of the world events that "he felt no loyalty whatever to any government, people, or country." And I've had newsmen tell me to my face in discussions like this: "Look, a story is a story is a story." That's what we in Defense have a little concern about. Because Defense Department representatives involved with this matter are concerned that there are going to be situations in which high resolution imagery from space, available in near-real-time, could pose national security problems by putting the lives of U.S. military personnel directly and immediately at risk, and that's what we're concerned about. Those are the kinds of situations with which we're concerned. Freedom of the press does not mean that just because a reporter comes in and asks for them, the classified plans for a sensitive military operation need be taken out of the safe and turned over to him. And the last-minute preparations in the field for the launching of such an operation in our view can be just as classified as those papers in the safe. That's what we're hoping to be able to protect.

What the media probably would describe as illegal prior restraint the Defense Department tends to view as denial of access of classified information. From my viewpoint and the talks I have around the Pentagon, Defense is fully cognizant of the importance of the First Amendment and its provision for freedom of the press. Defense has no intent to work in a capricious manner, but Defense also considers that a basic purpose for adoption of the United States Constitution went beyond the First Amendment and, as stated in the Preamble, was to provide for the common defense, and the Defense Department is the vehicle by which that common defense is provided.

The most immediate aspect of the situation that existence of a high quality commercial imaging capability in space would create for us relates to operations security. We recognize that we have a responsibility to protect the national security by what we call OPSEC, or Operation Security. If we want to protect the design of a radical new airplane, it's up to us to keep it under cover when a high resolution imaging satellite is within range. But there are going to be problems. We're convinced of this. There are going to be problems where OPSEC won't work, and that's why we're happy, reasonably happy, that is, with the present rules that the Department of Commerce promulgated in August. I could cite some possible situations but they would really be hypothetical, just exactly that. But you can dream up situations of your own in which it would be important to protect the national security. What puts teeth in the 1984 act is that the Secretary of Defense has the role of determining when national security is involved and of recommending to the Secretary of Commerce that restrictions be imposed.

We should keep in mind, though, that in promulgating the rules, the Department of Commerce included this statement in the supplementary information. And I'm quoting from Part 2 titled, "The First Amendment and National Security Concerns."

The National Oceanic and Atmospheric Administration recognizes that its licensing authority is subject to all constitutional and statutory safeguards and it is committed to exercising this authority with full regard for the First Amendment rights of all applicants and licensees including the press. The Act requires NOAA to consult with the Departments of Defense and State on all matters affecting national security and foreign policy interests.

In response to NOAA's request for consultation on these regulations, both departments have stated they will not require NOAA to impose any restriction on remote sensing activities that is not essential for national security purposes or to meet international obligations.

No provision in these rules or any action implementing the Land Remote-Sensing Commercialization Act of 1984 is intended to detract in any way from the First Amendment rights of any person including any organization which engages in news gathering and dissemination. National security, foreign policy, and international considerations will not be invoked as a basis for taking any action adverse to the interests of licensees unless the remedy is necessary and effective under existing judicial standards.

And there the matter rests. To my mind that goes a long, long way toward meeting the concerns that were expressed and the arguments that led up to the issuance of these rules. If a situation should arise in which imagery from space could put important national security interests at risk, I fully expect that the Department of Defense will seek denial of access on an immediate basis. A beforehand restriction is what that would be. The damage would have been done once the imagery is disclosed. If no imagery is obtained there's no problem of premature disclosure. I'm not aware, and I must admit to start with, I'm not a lawyer, but I'm not aware from my reading of any First Amendment court cases in which denial of access to classified information was the issue, particularly cases in which the action under litigation would have multiplied the casualties of U.S. personnel, and directly denied the chance of attaining an important and immediate national security objective. Whether any situation like that will ever arise, you can only speculate. I don't know. But if and when a commercially operated, high-resolution, near-real-time capability becomes available, I'm sure that space policy decisions will have to be newly addressed, and I'm sure that we will have court action if denial of access is implemented. Even as we meet today, the existing national space policy is under review. It's my understanding that the reviewers have not yet reached any decision relating to the time period when a top quality, high resolution mediasat will be available. But even when that day comes, I doubt very much that the basic goals of United States space policy will need to be changed much. The present six basic goals of the United States space policy are these: strengthen the security of the United States, maintain United States space leadership, retain economic and scientific benefits through the exploitation of space, expand United States private sector investment and involvement in civil space and space-related activities, promote international cooperative activities that are in the national interest, and cooperate with other nations in maintaining the freedom of space for all activities that enhance the security and the welfare of mankind. Within that existing policy, we think there's a lot that can be done.

QUESTIONS AND ANSWERS

Moderator: Larry, Jack said that the Department of Defense was fully cognizant of First Amendment rights as it relates to this issue. Do you agree with that?

Scharff: No, I don't think they're sensitive, if that's what he means about cognizant of First Amendment rights. I think there are a numler of misconceptions about what's involved here.

The notion that this is just classified information that the government has in its files that it can decide whether to release under the Freedom of Information Act or not, just a statutory decision for the government to make, is wrong. This is not information solely within the control of the government. This is information that is out there and that the media already have or will shortly have through the normal activity of their news-gathering process, without any aid from the government. The media don't need the assistance of the government as they would if asking for files. Therefore, it's not like classified information. It requires, in effect, a prior restraint by the government to stop it from being disseminated. That is not to say that the news media are insensitive to the national security interest here. I have tried to emphasize that they are, that there's usually cooperation, as in the case of Grenada, which he gave as an example. News media organizations did know about the preparations for the invasion and voluntarily withheld information. This would always be the case with so-called responsible organizations when they agreed with the government. There would be times when responsible organizations would not agree with the government. There would be times when irresponsible organizations would not agree with the government. We are not saying "trust us." We are saying that there is a mechanism that has been used for years if the government knows that something is about to be released which is a direct, serious, and an immediate threat to the national security. You go to court. You get a restraining order, and the government has time to do this. They can call up a judge at any time and get a restraining order if what the facts that they allege *ex parte* are sufficient to convince that judge that there is controversy here that he needs time to study before permitting the release of this information so that it is out of the bag.

I don't really think we have a quarrel except over the procedure by which the government goes about stopping this. I think what General Thomas is suggesting is that the government is in a position to know best and that it can make up its mind without going to a court, and when it does make up its mind, it can act unilaterally, and that is what. . . .

Moderator: Jack, do you want to respond to that? I think what Larry's saying is that the courts really ought to be the arbitrator and not the Department of State.

Thomas: The law says the Secretary of Defense will determine when national security interests are involved. There is no intention in the Department of Defense to act on its own. We have courts. We're concerned about very, very tight timing situations, and I didn't talk about procedures because they haven't really been determined yet. But certainly, in any situation in which we have time to go court and get a restraining order, I would expect that would occur. The Defense Department is not running off on its own like this, but it has some concerns. And one of the things that Mr. Scharff points out is most of the time the media do certain things, or most of the media agencies can be depended on. It's those others that we don't want to subject ourselves to risk from in very tight situations. We're not talking about everybody, but we want to have a system in which we do not have to depend on voluntary cooperation when we feel it's important that something be accomplished, and that's the position from which we work.

Question: . . . in any situation, though, you have no control, the Defense Department would have no control on foreign satellites passing over that same site where the commandos are getting ready for their instantaneous raid, and that information would be available worldwide except to U.S. media, wouldn't it?

Thomas: There is no commercial foreign system today that has a near-real-time, high-resolution capability. Mention has been made about Soyuz Karta. Soyuz Karta is prepared to disseminate information except on areas of the Soviet Union, on areas of Eastern Europe, or other areas that they don't want to sell imagery on. Let me tell you one little example to illustrate why we're not concerned about it.

An American group was in Russia and one of them tried to buy some Soviet photos. They were told: "Fine, how many do you want? We like to sell them in large groups. Tell us how many you want and when you need them, because we need to have enough of an order to enable us to go out and lay on a mission." The American said: "I just want to buy one." "No way." But then since he was a publisher of a U.S. magazine, he talked them into selling him one picture for $1,000 because he said, "We'll give you a story that advertises what you're doing." His picture was of Portland, Oregon. We don't consider that the kind of photography that Soyuz Karta is willing to sell, and its timeliness, gives us any concern. And what we are thinking about, also, is that we don't see any market for any of those foreign companies that would stimulate them into going into high resolution, near-real-time reporting. That's not where their market is.

Question: General, what about their intelligence agencies? Don't they have any incentive to develop this technology?

Thomas: Of course, they do.

Question: Are we always going to be superior to them, they're not going to be able to match us?

Thomas: No, I'm not saying that at all. But foreign intelligence services are not publishing their product. They are not making it available to anyone else.

Question: They could use it for military.

Thomas: There's no question they could use it to their own benefit the same as they can now.

Question: What about a commando raid, why aren't they going to respond to that?

Thomas: What would they do? We're not talking about a commando raid on the USSR. If we recognize that it's something directly involving interests of the USSR, as we do at the present time now, we would make efforts to do things at a time when they are not able to image it. You cannot have your satellites everywhere in the world all the time. And there are gaps. There are time phasings that can be taken advantage of. Let's put it this way: Suppose we could time phase an operation so that the Soviet satellites wouldn't see us, but that would put us within the imaging capability of a U.S. mediasat. We would want to be able to at least protect against any U.S. mediasat by denial of access and use timing as a means of protecting against Soviet imaging. I'm not saying these problems are easy. We may never solve them, I don't know. But we feel there's a big stake in trying to.

I am Bob Sherliff, from HBO. We've stated that remote sensing imagery is used for the purposes of national security and that the news gathering organizations are interested in using that for the purposes, or under the auspices of freedom of the press. As some people in this room know, HBO has scrambled their signals within the last two years, and we found that for the purpose of our own security, even the scrambling of those signals was somehow cracked by just some computer hack. My question is even though I'm sure these high resolution technologies are scrambled, how certain are we that these aren't subject to interception by unfriendly foreign interests that would compromise the national security that they're designed to protect?

Thomas: No more certain than we are about the security of any communications. One of the big games in the world among intelligence organizations is the race to crack codes and devise new ones, and then crack those. You're ahead sometimes and you're behind sometimes. I don't offer any guarantee that any kind of encryption system that would protect imagery could not be cracked.

I'm Dan Brenner, from UCLA. I'll direct it to Larry, although I have a very hard time understanding why foreign private enterprise or state-run enterprises like Spot would not provide the identical service that mediasat or ABC would.

Scharff: There's no demonstrated market there yet. That's the key thing. One of the things that could happen, of course, is that someone's willing to put up $100 million to pay for it.

Brenner: I think that's a question that maybe the market will determine for us. One problem is a legal question that I have for Larry—let me give a hypothetical—sometimes I'm permitted to do as a law professor and see how you'd handle it. Here we are. It's the two o'clock CNN headline newscast, and all of a sudden there's "let's go see what's up on the satellite today," and all of a sudden, the satellite is feeding pictures to CNN direct without any review. We know that happened in terms of an emergency when Sadat was assassinated. The pictures were coming over automatically without editing by the three networks. All of sudden, lo and behold, no one expected it. All of a sudden the satellite is picking up something. Now you anticipate a prior restraint hearing to permit the government to make its case that there's a national security interest, and under those circumstances there wouldn't be an opportunity for the government to know that you had something before it had been distributed on television. How would that scenario play out?

Scharff: Because I think there would be an opportunity before that. As I was saying before, the orbit of the satellite under the Landsat Act has to be provided to the government. The government will know just exactly where the satellite will be rotating, will know what sensitive activities it might be conducting at a particular time and place that the satellite might be coinciding with, and will have the opportunity to go to court even before you know that that's what's going to be seen, and that's also my answer to the hypotheticals that the general gave before about troop preparations or rescue preparations or whatever. If they know that they're going to be doing something in an area that the satellite is going over, they will have plenty of opportunity to go to court.

Michael Schubert, San Diego State University: Running throughout your comments has been the idea of real time capability, and also you mentioned the very short action/reaction time legally. If I put two and two together from your comments, are you implying that we can look forward to some sort of a time delay/prior restraint mechanism?

Thomas: It could be. That's one solution, yes. I'm not sure that these situations ever will arise, but if they arise, that is one solution.

Schubert: And if the government asks for such a solution, how would the media representatives, Larry, react to that?

Scharff: It would be dependent on, just as I was saying before, if the media representatives acted the way I would expect them to act in the case of preparing for an invasion of Grenada or rescue operation, they would say, of course, we're going to keep this secret. And if they don't agree to that, or the government has any reason not to trust them, they can go to court.

Thomas: I mentioned at one time a journalist had told me to my face "a story is a story is a story." It was when I gave him a hypothetical incident, just as you're describing here. He said, "Of course, we'd go with it. A story is a story is a story." That's why I had qualms occasionally.

Scharff: Could I ask a real quick question and maybe this is just a partial quotation, but in the *New York Times* of October 13, Fred Iklé, undersecretary of defense for policy, was quoted as saying. . . .

Thomas: He was misquoted, so I was advised.

Scharff: He was quoted as saying there was no problem with civilian remote sensing.

Thomas: And his staff assistant told me he was quoted out of context. That's all I know, because I was not there. I don't know.

Brenner: What was the quote, Larry? What was that misquote, I should say?

Scharff: Mr. Iklé was quoted as saying: "The notion has been around that the Pentagon might worry about high-powered civil satellites, but we have no concerns." He did not elaborate.

Moderator: Well, I thank our two panelists, and they'll be around, I think, for questions later.

NOTE

1. A revision of the National Space Policy released in February 1988 makes no mention of a limit on commercial imagery resolution.

6

The First Amendment—Rights of Privacy

Edwin H. James, Elliot E. Maxwell, Tony Acone, and Fred W. Weingarten

EDWIN H. JAMES

So now we come to privacy in the age of high tech, and I want you to know I've been thinking about this for twenty-five years. At a luncheon in Washington, I was sitting next to a Victor A. Sholis, who was at that time running the stations then owned by the *Courier Journal* in Louisville, Kentucky, a guy with a pretty sharp wit. The speaker of the day was talking about the future of satellites, which were then not only a novelty but merely a sort of an idea in space. And when he got to the point of predicting that there would be satellites swinging around up there with cameras that could take high-resolution pictures in great detail, Sholis turned to me and said, "Excuse me, I've got to go home and clean up the backyard." Privacy was already an issue in a space age that had barely begun.

Actually, I'm here with some reluctance because discussing the right of privacy these days can get pretty dangerous. Judge Bork would agree with me if he were here and so would Judge Ginsburg if he had stayed around long enough to go through that nomination proceeding. I expect *Roe* v. *Wade* to come out in paperback pretty soon. But as was evident in the unfortunate Judge Bork's hearing, rights of privacy are often in dispute and subject to shifts in culture and opinion. Franklin Delano Roosevelt served as President for three terms and the beginning of the fourth, and nobody ever mentioned that he had a mistress. In Jack Kennedy's shorter term as president and as a senator beforehand, he was totally spared news coverage of his occasional ventures in strange hay. I imagine Gary Hart longs for the good old days. For public figures, especially those in or aspiring to elective office, private privilege is fading fast, but more about that later. Before we speculate on how collisions may occur in the future between the First Amendment and the right of privacy, a brief inspection of the wreckage left by collisions up to date may be useful. It is not a tidy scene. Privacy is not among the rights to be found in the Constitution or its amendments. It is among the rights that the first Congress is presumed to have had in mind when it wrote the Ninth Amendment, which reads: "the enumeration in the Constitution of certain rights shall not be construed to deny or disparage others retained by the people." The courts have also found a right of privacy implied in the Fourteenth Amendment, adopted in 1868, which says that no law may "abridge the privileges or immunities of citizens of the United States" and that no state may "deprive any person of life, liberty, or property without due process of law." Privacy has become a legal right defined in the statutes of most states, and it can outweigh the news media's First Amendment rights in certain circumstances.

As explained in a discussion of the subject by a useful publication issued by the Reporter's Committee for Freedom of the Press, privacy law has developed into four branches: unreasonable intrusion into the seclusion of another; public disclosure of private facts; placing a person in a false light in the public eye; and misappropriation of a name or a likeness for commercial gain. As the Supreme Court has said, "There *is* [and the court italicized *is*], There *is* a zone of privacy surrounding every individual, a zone within which the state may protect him from intrusion by the press with all its attendant publicity."

In the case before the court at that time, WSB-TV Atlanta was held to have been safely outside the zone when it identified the victim of a rape and murder despite a Georgia law prohibiting the identification of victims of rape. The station's defense was that its reporter had obtained the name from indictments on public file in a court where the victim's assailants were to be sentenced. The court upheld that position, saying the state may not "impose sanctions on the accurate publication of the name of a rape victim obtained from public records, more specifically, from judicial records that are maintained in connection with a public prosecution and which themselves are open to public inspection." The court, however, explicitly refrained from any finding on the constitutionality of the state's forbidding access in the first instance by the public or the press to some kinds of official records, those of a juvenile court, for example.

What else may be outside the zone of privacy? Or inside the zone? Last year the Supreme Court let stand a jury award of $1,500 actual damages and $25,000 punitive damages to a 16-year-old who had been correctly identified by the *Greenville News* (South Carolina) as the father of an illegitimate child. The plaintiff's experience had been reported as part of a long piece on teen-age pregnancies. So you're safe to identify a rape victim in Atlanta, even if state law explicitly prohibits identification, as long as the name is on public view in court. But it can cost you $26,500 in Greenville, South Carolina, to report the unchallenged fact that an adolescent became a father out of wedlock.

An invasion of privacy could have been turned into a much more expensive proposition for journalists if a jury in New York had been given its way. A couple of years ago a jury awarded $1,250,000 for the invasion of the privacy of a man who was interviewed by WCBS-TV New York. The plaintiff in the case, a man in his seventies, was caught by a WCBS-TV correspondent and camera crew as he emerged from his factory, which was next to property where barrels of toxic waste had been found. He objected to the presence of the camera, but he said, "We didn't dump them," when asked how the barrels got there. That clip was put on the air. He sued for libel, slander, trespass, assault and invasion of privacy, losing on the first four but prevailing on the last. WCBS-TV officials denied that it was an ambush interview, which they defined as a pursuit of a recalcitrant subject who is known to be evading interviews. The jury obviously thought otherwise. Its members saw an elderly man cornered by a camera. Their verdict was a reminder that 40 percent of the respondents in a poll conducted a year or two before that for the American Society of Newspaper Editors (ASNE), and otherwise favorable to television, had agreed that television news "invades people's privacy." This was a subject which you heard David Laventhol of Times Mirror discuss at lunch today, and it's a very serious one. Public attitudes toward the media are not as favorable in some respects as the media would like, but that's another issue, one that insinuates itself into almost any discussion when you're talking about rights of privacy. That jury award in New York was overturned by the U.S. Court of Appeals for the Second Circuit in New York which said, "A court cannot substitute its judgment for that of the press to present an article or broadcast in what the court believes is a balanced manner. It may only assess liability when the press so oversteps its editorial freedom that it contains falsity and does so with a requisite degree of fault."

I digress here to mention that the First Amendment, especially in libel cases, has found far more friends in recent years among judges of appellate courts than it has among trial juries, and I think that is a condition that goes back to the question of invasion of people's privacy that was found by that 40 percent response to the ASNE poll.

Now the appellate verdict in New York brings us to the subject of malice, which is a common defense in contemporary libel actions and a defense in invasion of privacy suits as well. This was when the court said unless the press so oversteps its editorial freedom that it contains falsity and does so with the requisite degree of fault.

It also brings us to a distinction between public and private plaintiffs. To prevail in suits for libel or invasion of privacy, as we all probably know, public figures must prove that the account at issue was false and that the defendant published or broadcast it with knowledge of its falsity or with reckless disregard of whether it was true or false. As discussed by the Supreme Court in 1974, in a case accusing the *Cleveland Plain Dealer* of invasion of privacy, malice may be proved by a private plaintiff theretofore outside the public eye on a showing that the defendant bore ill will toward the plaintiff or proceeded with "wanton disregard of the plaintiff's rights." Now there's a big distinction there between the private application of malice and the public figure's definition.

That private standard seems to me to provide some shelter for private persons of the future who would object to, say, the publication or broadcast of their bank balances as contained in the computers of a credit clearing house. Unless, of course, the courts decide that computer records of that kind constitute public records, in which case Nelly bar the door. As an editor I do not feel grievously deprived if private bank balances stay private, except, of course, those belonging to people of genuine news interest and legitimately at issue in the news. Let's just say that as technology makes it possible to store, retrieve, and move information around in great quantities and at speeds approaching that of light, there will be plenty of work for lawyers specializing in the law of privacy and the First Amendment.

ELLIOT E. MAXWELL

I should make it clear at the outset that my remarks do not necessarily reflect the views of my company, Pacific Telesis; where they do, it is a happy confluence and where they do not, this allows them to disavow my words.

There was a remark made earlier today that this was the twentieth anniversary of Sergeant Pepper. I'd like to harken back for a moment to the same time period and the song "Mrs. Robinson" from *The Graduate*. In that song it says, "We'd like to know a little more about you for our files." I think that sets a useful tone for this particular panel, because what we're facing is the possibility, not the certainty, but the possibility, of the accumulation and manipulation of large amounts of data about millions of individuals.

Such a possibility has important consequences for the right of privacy, as well as First Amendment considerations.

Mr. James has talked about the First Amendment side of it, but I'd like to go back and bring us up from that summer of love to the last three months, to focus a bit more on what's happening and what's possible in accumulating data on individuals. I'd like to key off the last thing he said, which was that, as an editor, he's not so interested in the bank balances of people who are not public figures. The negative pregnant there is that we are interested in the bank balances of public figures. One example of this occurred during the Bork nomination hearings when someone went to the local video store that Mr. Bork frequented and said, "I'd like to know what videos he has rented, and I'd like to put this in my paper." Someone then gave the reporter the information. The question this raises is whether it is appropriate for the newspaper to solicit or to receive or to publish, and for the local video store to provide, this information about any individual, whether public or private.

What was the upshot of this? It is a paradigm of the Washington public policy process that (a) the newspaper when hunting parenthetically found nothing of much interest, and (b) several days later there was a bill introduced called The Video Privacy Act of 1987, which would forbid this activity and provide up to $10,000 in damages. The general public disapproval of the publication of this information and the introduction of this bill reflects what is perceived as a broad societal concern about privacy. This is overwhelmingly confirmed by public opinion polls.

All this must be viewed in the context of rapidly developing technology. Technology now permits the relatively inexpensive maintenance and manipulation of great masses of data. Technology may even change how we think about different kinds of information. In the past, as Mr. James described it, a reporter could simply say, "This is a public record and therefore I can use it." But if you are now able to pull all public records together and manipulate them, is there a cause for worry? There were, in fact, questions raised when the press in Rhode Island took all of the public mortgage records, put them together, and said, "This shows a pattern of corruption." There are good reasons to think that that's just what the press should do. But I have a nagging feeling that if a newspaper could put all public records together in a database, we'd all feel a little uncomfortable because so much so-called public information would be readily available about us.

We do have to recognize that the gathering of information often serves very useful purposes. For example, the telephone company collects a fair amount of data because they bill people on a per call basis for toll calls. So the telephone company knows when a call is made and by whom and to whom and the respective locations of the parties. Now it has an option. Obviously, it could choose not to gather and use that data. When my wife was in Germany, she used to get a phone bill that had one line that said, "You owe 'X' amount for your phone bill." That's all she received. Now would we be comfortable with that? Is that all the information we would like to have? There are, obviously, trade-offs about transaction data that's collected. If I order something, I like to make sure that the order is correct, that it's the right piece of merchandise, so in case I have any question about the bill, I can check that information. That tends to increase the collection and maintenance of data.

There is also a tendency for those who have such data to gather even more in order to be able to more effectively market their services. If I gather more data, I may be able to serve you better. I may be able to give you things that you want. I may be able to call you on the phone and say, "I know that this is the kind of thing that you've been buying in the past. Would you like to buy some more?" And you might feel very good that someone calls you because that's exactly the kind of product you want. Now, is that intrusive? It seems likely that people will think it less intrusive when someone supplies them more efficiently with what they want. On the other hand, if you don't want that phone call, it may seem very intrusive and it might increase how much you worry about the accumulation of data. So, at the same time that we are saying we are worried about data collection, we are sending a different signal with our purchase decisions. And that different signal is that it is okay to gather data and use it to sell goods and services.

There are other examples of competing interests. Today's AIDS crisis captures some of the real dilemmas. In the best of all possible worlds it might be useful to be able to say a person has AIDS and to be able to let others know for treatment purposes. But the information is not neutral. This isn't the best of all possible worlds. People have legitimate concerns about things such as discrimination in employment and social stigmatization if the information were made public.

What this leads to is why we worry about privacy at all. We're worried about it, as I said, because of questions of employment, questions of credit worthiness, questions about how we will be treated. One of our great justices called privacy "the right most precious to civilized man," in part because privacy allows people to experiment, to dissent, to be nonconforming, to have around them a zone in which they can behave as they want without any concern about societal judgments.

What the right of privacy does in protecting that freedom to be nonconforming was, in the past, the function of the frontier in the United States. People used to be able to go to the frontier and take on a new identity. Now you can't escape your past by going West, because someone will call an agency back East to have them look up your file. And your concern about privacy reflects our desire, as the same justice wrote, "to be left alone."

The First Amendment rubs up against this right, as Mr. James has described. It is hard to resolve the competing interests. During Watergate the first link between the White House and the Watergate burglars was disclosed in phone records that were obtained in violation of telephone company policy. That privacy violation allowed people to begin tracing the involvement of the White House in Watergate. The result might be laudable; but I'm glad that the telephone company has a policy that says people are subject to dismissal for release of exactly that kind of information. There's even a state law in California which says one cannot make available such information about subscribers without due process of law. Another example from more recent times of the tension between First Amendment rights and privacy rights is the *New York Times* sending a questionnaire to all of this year's presidential candidates that said, "Please send me your medical records, your mental health records, a list of your friends past and present, and a waiver of your privacy rights." We need to look carefully at the tension between the right of privacy and the First Amendment, but I do not believe that there's any principle that one can draw, or any bright line, that will ultimately reconcile these two things. I think they will be balanced and analyzed again and again in specific circumstances.

Most of the tensions between the First Amendment and the right of privacy involve public figures. We also need to look carefully at the right of privacy of people who are not public figures and see how we can protect it given our technological prowess. One model for treating data accumulation is the common carrier model that governs the phone company. Under this model, both the substance of the communication and the facts surrounding it are held as private and are not available to others. There are severe penalties for disclosure. A similar model comes from the Cable Act, which forbids the disclosure of subscriber data. Another form of regulation is found in the Fair Credit Reporting Act, which is based upon the propositions that people need to have access to their files, that people need to be able to make corrections to their files, and that there should be limits as to who can receive the information that is collected.

There are obviously other ways of thinking about privacy. One theory supports self-regulation. Marketing organizations argue that economics will impel them to act properly. Their theory is that if they harass people, then people aren't going to buy from them. And if they behave well, they are going to be economically rewarded. Under this theory, regulation other than self-regulation is unnecessary.

There are different models abroad that may ultimately affect data practices in the United States. Most of these models are highly regulatory. They even assume the regulation of private databases. In 1984 in Great Britain, for example, a law was passed that said, in effect, that if you had a computerized list to generate Christmas cards for over sixty people, you had to register the list with the government. You would be subject to damages for misuse of the list or for using it for purposes for which it was not registered. I don't believe that we will carry regulation to this extent, but it is a useful lesson in that we have traditionally underestimated the secondary effects of regulation.

Other models also rely more heavily on damages. The Privacy Act in the United States provides for actual damages. In Canada, there is unlimited liability for entities such as the telephone company for misuse of data.

To close, I would point you in the direction of work that Arthur Miller has done about privacy. He gives us a way of looking at privacy, and he describes how people should behave if they are the keeper of the data. I should note that as I look around at the group here, I see a number of media organizations that hold substantial amounts of data about people. There are newspaper morgues that contain huge bodies of information about individuals and groups. Media organizations often have information based upon private transactions. So Miller's advice may be useful to you, not only as you think about the conflicts between privacy and the First Amendment, but as you maintain and utilize the data you collect.

Miller suggests that there are five duties that the database manager has. One is the duty of care, which essentially is don't be negligent with the data you collect. Don't be foolish about them. Be careful with them. A second duty is to exercise restraint in what kind of information is requested. You shouldn't take in more than you need, because if you take in more than you need, you are unlikely to be very careful with it. A third duty is to make the information system and the data secure. That may involve back-up data or access controls on the data or audit tracks—all things that the technology can now provide to you. The fourth duty is to make sure that people have access to their files and can make corrections in the data.

The last duty is an especially interesting one. Miller describes it as providing death to data. What he says is that data are like people. Data get born. They grow. And they get linked or married to other data that he describes as holy data lock. And more files get born or spawned. Finally the data grow old. What is different is that data seldom ever die. The important thing is to be able to kill the data because they can get more dangerous. So he ends with an appeal for death to data. As we sit here in the year of the Irangate Hearings, I'm sure that Ollie North and Fawn Hall would have been very glad to know that a Harvard professor supported the idea of destroying data. Interesting, isn't it?

TONY ACONE

I met Elliot last night for the first time at the cocktail party. We had a chance to compare notes on our approaches to this panel this afternoon. For some strange reason he and I made similar comments. So some of what I'm going to say may be a little bit redundant. I am not going to say much of it because my baseball days tell me that in batting third the guy who was third, especially when there were two outs, wanted to avoid an out so that the clean-up hitter could get up there. I think you all are, in fact, the clean-up hitter and your questions and comments will contribute the important conclusion to the discussion. I think the subject is important to us, especially in this area of the public figure. Although we think in terms of public figures as being those either declared as candidates for public office or who are now officials in the political context, I certainly know and have had to deal with public figures in the entertainment business. I have, in fact, been reminded on occasion that my experience in front of cameras might very well constitute making me a public figure. And so those particular questions and issues that we are discussing produce a certain sobering feeling. As an executive of a cable system that gathers data of the type Elliot referred to, we are asked to deal constantly with that data, and sometimes to avoid dealing with it, these issues as I say give one that sobering feeling.

I'm reminded of a time when I first got into the cable business in 1967. I was pleased to gain employment at Leisure World up in Laguna Hills, and I used to do a daily sports show at 3:00 every afternoon on the local channel that was carried on the cable system serving the Leisure World community. We had a reception some months after I had begun this assignment. At this reception I met many of the residents of the community. I had an interesting conversation with one of those residents who informed me that his wife did not turn on the television set at 3:00 P.M. unless she made sure that her hair was properly coiffed, that her dress was something that she didn't mind being seen in, and that her entire demeanor was proper. I found that to be a little strange, a little different, and I inquired as to some of the reasons for being so careful. He said, because I always closed my show with "I'll see you tomorrow," and this dear woman was firmly convinced that if she turned on her TV set, although she was looking at me, she was sure that I could see her.

That was twenty years ago, and interestingly enough, with the data that has been collected, with this access to a great deal of information that we have in the cable television business, by God, we have a pretty good view of the people out there. And that's really what previous speakers, and certainly Elliott, were referring to. Questions about what movies you watch, what pay per view events do you choose, what books you read, what hospital records concerning you are available. All this is of significant importance—the word AIDS was a new word to me about five years ago. I first heard it on the golf course playing a quick nine holes with a friend of mine who is an oncologist. We somehow got on the subject of herpes and he said, "Tony, let me tell you something. Herpes is going to be much like having the measles in a number of years because we are going to realize an epidemic that is just going to be something fantastic and it's going to be called AIDS." He began to tell me about this dread disease. In the conversation he cited that one of the great problems occurs when a physician suspects that an individual might have AIDS. He must then secure a specific release by that patient to run a test to confirm or deny that the person in fact had AIDS. This opens the whole subject of intrusion into particular records of a hospital's files for a "potential public figure" because if a person declares that he intends to seek public office the rights to the information about him could be available to the media. We've spoken quite a bit today about the people's right to know. What about the government's right to know about the people, about us on a one-on-one basis? These are questions of serious concern.

The law in California, I think, is pretty explicit in denying the right by a cable operator to release any information that could be identified with a specific individual. In fact we, as a cable television association, were so zealous in our seeking such legislation for that protection that we found it ironic that all of a sudden when it came time to try to prosecute someone for piracy of cable television service, the legislation was turned against us. The individual was a basic subscriber and paying his bills so we knew who he was. He was stealing a pay TV service. We found in trying to prosecute, that we could not identify the person. He was protected by the right of privacy. The law was subjected to some modification and efforts to prosecute pirates can now be carried out.

The thought occurs to me that if, in fact, some believe that there is no need for franchising and that anybody can willy nilly just go out and build a cable system there will clearly be chaos. If a government agency franchises a company to operate a cable system, I guess it's assumed that the franchisee must follow certain rules imposed by the franchising agency including the right to privacy of those subscribers to the system. The thought then occurs to me that if I come in and build a Satellite Master Antenna Television system, for instance, and in doing so I am not franchised by a government agency, wouldn't it be correct that someone subscribing to my service should, in fact, be concerned. Quite frankly, I am going to be able to gather similar, if not the same, data as any government franchised company would be gathering. As a subscriber to that particular service, shouldn't I be concerned as to the retention of that information and the protection of my right to privacy? So I pose that question in support of local government being the franchising agency. The local government then must make the decision as to whether or not they desire for whatever reason to grant an additional franchise. The phrase "exclusivity of franchise" was mentioned a number of times today. I don't know that any franchise that we have, that we operate under, has any exclusivity to it, and so I leave you with that particular thought and I appreciate the opportunity of being here.

QUESTIONS AND ANSWERS

Moderator: Our panel would be happy to welcome any questions you might have on the right of privacy as it relates to the First Amendment. Marilyn—

I am Marilyn Huff, and I'm with the law firm of Gray Cary Ames & Frye.

I want to direct the panel's attention to the topic that Ed James brought up, and one of the categories was the public disclosure of private facts. I would like your input on what a news media person should do in this scenario. Suppose that a news media person discovers that a candidate running for public office has AIDS. Does it make a difference to you whether the candidate is running for president of the United States, is running for a state legislative office, or is running for a school board position? Do you feel any constraints on the media's right to publish this information and, if so, what are the public policy considerations that you have?

Ed James: I think you have to be practical about it. First, legally, you're a lawyer I'm told and probably a very good one, so I should not get into legal questions at all because I'm not a lawyer. As an editor I would say that if he were a presidential candidate, there is no question in my mind that it's a free ball. If I were the editor of a local daily in a city small enough for many people to know that person, and a school board job were at stake and a matter of considerable local interest, I think I would want to do the same thing. It's a question of what news value you attach to it, and at that point, you're on very thin ice because we have very few standards that you can resort to aside from those of common sense, experience, and general good taste and judgment, all of which are imperfect standards to go by. I don't know how to answer that except to say you have to make the judgment as to whether the revelation of that information is of significant use to the community or the electorate. If it's some minor figure, I would wonder about whether you want to wreck his life.

Tony Acone: I guess I'd have to say if it's important at any level, why is it not important at every level? I would say the school board level of someone seeking office is certainly of utmost importance to those taking the time and the interest to go to the voter's box and vote, and certainly to those paying taxes to support that school district. I think the item posed earlier this morning might fit here. I forget who discussed the situation regarding a particular student body of kids that was being allowed or disallowed to wear a particular T-shirt advertising something on it. The school took exception. To that youngster, that was as important as the First Amendment could be. He was being denied the right to express himself and if that runs true, and I think it might, then I don't know that there exists any different degree of importance, if you weighed the presidency versus the local school board candidate.

Moderator: Elliot, I know you wanted to add something to this.

Elliot Maxwell: The classic question was posed to Floyd Abrams about what does the press do in the following circumstance, and he answered, which seemed to be probably the only good answer, "it depends." I don't think I would agree that if it's important to one person, it's important to everyone, because if you took the chain down from president to school board officials, is it important to the person next door that you discover they have AIDS and therefore it should be made public? And I would say, no. And there is at some point that the societal interests versus the interests in the privacy of that person's condition come into balance. But that's going to be a judgment call, and I don't think there is any good rule about it, but one has to, I think, acknowledge, and sometimes I think people in the press because of the concern of that encroachment on the First Amendment have to acknowledge that there is a privacy interest that people have and treat that with a certain amount of dignity, because, in fact, the First Amendment and the honor it receives is in part dependent upon it being in play with other interests, rather its national security interests or privacy. That one can take absolute positions, but eventually absolute positions don't work.

Moderator: Removing the press for just a minute on that, Elliott, let's go back to your person-next-door comment. Would your opinion change for a person who desired to date the individual?

Elliot Maxwell: It seems to me that it changes the question entirely because the press is saying this is information that I will make available to the public at large. If someone is going to be dating, one imagines that probably there should be some talk between the person to be dated and the person who is dating. If that doesn't happen then, I think that there's probably going to be trouble in the relationship anyway. But the press thing adds a very different dimension, and that's what you have to then say, is this, because one doesn't publish essentially to one, one publishes to everybody or makes available to everyone. And so I think at that point one does balance, and as I said, it depends.

Moderator: Are there any other questions?

Question: A question on high tech versus privacy. Some 55 miles from here, in this building, at 11:00 at night, a terrible noise is heard in the house. I think an express train is about to go through, I get up out of bed, (there's a bedroom on the second floor) and the window I go to overlooks a grassy bank. There is a police helicopter going around with his light shining. Second pass, I'm a little groggy, but at the second pass down comes the light into the bedroom and I'm in a TV studio all of a sudden. I think with a VCR or camera up there they could have got some great pictures of the cat jumping around, but it was a bedroom and I ask the question, and it's happened in other instances, at what point does law enforcement or chasing or looking, where do you draw the line and do I have to go to bed and just close the blinds every night because there's going to be a helicopter up there wondering what I'm doing in my bedroom?

Elliot Maxwell: I could refer to Larry Scharff because we were talking about a case somewhat similar—although here you're not the object of the search. You're not the intended object of the search.

If there's a burglar wandering around somewhere, everybody is suspect.

Elliot Maxwell: There was a case in which the police had used a helicopter to fly over the backyard of someone who was growing marijuana, and the

Supreme Court had a tough job with that one 5 to 4. I frankly don't think they'd have a very tough job with a searchlight into your bedroom.

If one sort of analogizes, just because people get the data it doesn't mean they should be able to keep the data or make use of it. The answer is no, and that just because you're able at some point to do it, that's why you have a set of legal procedures. And the question in some ways has been, where does the government interest end and where the sort of control mechanism end, because that's the difference at the moment and the only recognition is that we are at a point where we have to be thinking about this and the steps, if any, beyond what we now have in place.

Moderator: We're fortunate to have another legal comment from the back of the room.

Question: Well, my comment isn't so much legal as opening up for discussion a couple of the points that you've made. I actually have two questions that I would like to ask. One is, given a zone of privacy that we as individuals like to protect, and as public individuals, perhaps a zone of publicity that surrounds us, do you think that zone should also extend to our spouses and our family? I throw out the examples of John Zaccaro, husband of the public figure Geraldine Ferraro, who is found to be involved in some real estate corruption because she particularly sought the vice-presidency, and on the other hand, Judge Ginsburg's wife who was suddenly discovered to have been performing abortions in her first year of residency. So my first question is, do you think that zone should extend to the immediate family of those public individuals, and then second, in particular regard of the press and what we've come to believe is very much a judgment call of the press on these privacy issues due to their First Amendment protection, do you think the fact that we have such an incredible competition between so many new press people, cable press, CNN, three major networks, and an abundance of newspaper outlets, do you think this competition has promoted them to act more loosely in these judgment calls and perhaps be a little bit more risky in making these judgment calls?

Elliot Maxwell: Answering your last question first the answer is yes, because competition encourages invigorated reporting. So it's more apt to encourage than discourage close judgment calls. I don't think it's irrelevant if families of candidates for high office are somehow found to be involved in a social act or whatever that is of some question is a matter perfectly legitimate to report. I don't think that the revelation of Ginsburg's wife's experience as a medical resident doing legal abortions had a goddamn thing to do with his disaster; neither did the marijuana smoking. These gave an excuse to the people who didn't want him in the first place on grounds that they hadn't been able quite to pin down because he hadn't written very much. The same people didn't want him on the court that didn't want Bork on the court and those provided enough impetus so that it was smart for him politically, and smart for the president politically, to say let's quit while we're not so far behind that we can't get anybody nominated. So I think you've got to leave it to the judgment of the people. We saw no big uproar where there may have been among some of the terribly militant, right-to-life people, but they would object to anything related to that sort of thing, and they would be people in his corner from the start. We saw no public outcry saying this woman is a terrible person because she did that. It was revealed and people said, so what? And as for John Zaccaro, he went through a whole court thing and finally was exonerated, the hard way, of one thing, but the press didn't indict him. He was indicted by fully constituted legal authority and went through a court trial.

Question: The beauty of an answer such as "it depends" is that it can get you out of anything. The thing that was most striking about the *New York Times*' request to the presidential candidates was that it says, tell me all your friends, past and present, and what it said was there's no attenuation. There is nothing that says at some point I'm not going to go out and talk to all these folks and say tell me everything you know about this person. If, in fact, a family member is involved in an illicit activity, then you probably would want to know it because you assume that the family member and the public figure have some kind of interchange. That's an assumption that's kind of a reasonable assumption. Maybe it's not true, but that at that level, you would say, that seems reasonable. At some point you say, no, that's so far distant that because they're related in some way to a public figure then I don't think you do it. It ought to be a judgment call.

Response: I think you ought to explain to the audience that the *New York Times* withdrew that request, and Max Frankel, the editor, said they'd gone much too far with it and gave an order to kill. It was never carried out. Only two people responded to it: Paul Simon and one other, and they both said, "Fine, we'll give you all the material." Frankel withdrew it and said he felt it had stepped over the bounds.

Response: I stand corrected. I didn't know that, but I think that's fine. But I think in some ways it was a kind of useful symbol.

FRED W. WEINGARTEN*

Before I start, I need to set forth a couple of caveats. In the first place, my comments are my own and don't represent those of my bosses—neither OTA, the Technology Assessment Board, nor the Congress.

Second, I am not a lawyer, much less a constitutional lawyer. I am a policy analyst with a computer science background. So, to avoid a useless (for me) debate over what is or is not a First Amendment issue, I will use

---

*A heavy snowstorm prevented Fred Weingarten from attending the conference in person. He did, however, submit this section that follows.

a surrogate for it in my comments, a societal and policy purpose that seems to me to underlie not only the First Amendment, but much other information law. In fact, so fundamental is this policy goal that we might consider the First Amendment, itself, might be considered to be the surrogate. It is one that is central to much information and communication policy in this country—the right of the people to know and to speak. To know what? Good question! It's not for me to decide. That's the point.

Information Policy and Technology

Information policy in this country arises out of conflict—conflict among the variety of values and purposes we attribute to information. There are no absolutes; no one value dominates all the time.

The balances among these values sometimes are achieved deliberately, as was the case, for instance, with the Electronic Communication Privacy Act, passed last year. One purpose of the act was to strike a considered balance between the right of individuals to communicate privately with each other and the duties of criminal justice agencies to enforce the law by collecting information about possible criminal activities. The act achieves this by allowing government wiretapping, but only under carefully controlled, court-supervised conditions.

In other instances, law has not seemed necessary. We have depended on the inefficiency, complexity, or cost of intrusion to protect us against widespread surveillance or abuse of privacy. For example, the difficulty of searching paper-based filing systems provided some degree of de facto information privacy for information that was theoretically in the public domain but in reality was buried in a musty basement below the county clerk's office.

Technology is now removing those inefficiencies of storage and retrieval and, thus, shifting old legislative balances, often away from privacy. Although, of course, I have my own personal views, it is less important to me as a policy analyst that balances be struck at any particular point than that we, as a democratic society, think about and debate these conflicts and establish balances carefully and deliberately, aware of the social, political, and economic implications for our society. What is most important in a democracy is that balances between competing fundamental social values be struck deliberately, through public debate. Otherwise, we risk letting technology define our society by default.

I propose that there are four values we attribute to information that often conflict with one another and, hence, need balancing. They are:

1. Privacy—the right to control access by others to information about oneself;
2. Property—the treatment of information as a marketable commodity;
3. Public—information as a resource readily available to the public;
4. Governance—the need for government entities to collect, store and use information to carry out its functions.

Information Technology and Privacy

Over the last several years, new information technologies, by offering us new capabilities or changing the effectiveness of old ones, have changed those balances of power. In the area of privacy, the tilting seems to have been mostly in the direction of those who want to collect and use information about people for whatever reason, and away from those who want to preserve privacy and autonomy.

Microelectronics provide a wide assortment of new *technologies for watching, listening, and following*—photographic eyes in space, miniature electronic microphones and television cameras, tiny radio tracers (so-called "bumper beepers"), and wiretapping devices.

Computers collect, organize, and store information about people. These information systems are sensitive not only because of the direct information they contain, but also because they can be used to develop elaborate profiles that infer other facts or predict behavior about the data subjects in them.

New communication systems allow information to be rapidly transferred around the world, accessible to anyone with a terminal and the ability to convince the computer that he or she is qualified to see it. Of course, these communication links are also supporting the proliferation of electronic mass media—some new, some old—through which the press could or does carry out its functions: videotext, television, radio, cable, optical disks, and so on.

Desk-top publishing potentially gives the power of the press to many more people, in a sense, returning to the colonial era of the penny press.

Finally, a *personal information marketplace*, growing rapidly, is composed of those who, for a wide variety of purposes, want to buy personal data of various kinds and those who find it profitable to collect, assemble, and sell it. The press plays both roles, as a potential source and as a potential customer of these data.

This is, by its very nature, part of the information infrastructure of our society; and, of course, it is subject to all of the technological and economic forces I just listed. So, it would be surprising if the press were not experiencing conflict. These trends are creating or exacerbating tensions that pit the public's right to know against other information values—tensions that will likely be difficult to resolve. One of the most important of these conflicts is with the person's right to privacy.

Conflict at Four Stages of Publishing

Conflicts between privacy and the First Amendment would occur at each of four stages of the publishing process.

Collection of Information

Clearly, it is the stage of collecting information that we think of first when we think of privacy; and, here, technology has dealt a strong hand to the collectors.

The problem is not only the availability of new surveillance tools mentioned above, but the basic changes in our information society. In this modern, computerized economy, we all are leaving behind us a bright electronic trail of information as we go about our daily lives. This trail is indelible; and, in many cases, it is openly available to anyone for a price. Even data that are not openly available can often easily be obtained. Most important, one doesn't have to be a prominent or public figure to leave that trail. We are all vulnerable.

Editorial Choice

It seems to me, and I assume to other observers, that the standards about what is publishable, about what is appropriate, relevant, and of legitimate public interest are shifting. Certainly many of my bosses in Congress seem to perceive such a shift in terms of politicians. Now it would be hard to argue that technology itself has been responsible for that shift in values. However, it may contribute to it in at least two subtle ways.

In the first place, as I have already argued, if there is simply more information available and the tools for probing more available, the press is able to examine more intimately. This ability suggests that borderline decisions are bound to arise more often. This is another one of those "protection by inefficiency" arguments. When information is very difficult to get (or even unavailable) you rarely need to ask whether it is appropriate to be published. Of course, again, this increase in information availability is probably greater for those not usually in the public eye, those who don't seek out public attention.

Secondly, technology seems to have presented us with a far more diverse and competitive structure of the industry loosely labeled "the press." This size and diversity would make any sort of agreement on boundaries extraordinarily difficult to establish and hold to. An editorial staff, when deciding whether to run a story, must take into account the possibility that some other publication may well choose to do so.

Of course, we all share the belief that competition and multiplicity of voices is a positive benefit to democracy. It is a basic goal of much communications policy in this country. However, a price we pay is that it does create pressures against privacy considerations.

Disseminating

The press has available an expanding variety of new technical means for delivering their product. Use of different media, of course, doesn't change whether something has been made public or not. It has been published, regardless. But media can certainly enhance the impact of the information.

Copy for national newspapers and wire service is transmitted over satellite and broadcast news is carried over world-wide communication facilities. Technology provides rapid global access to information that has been published. If, in the old days the swiftest horse could not catch up with the fastest-traveling word, these days not even the swiftest jet can outrace its speed-of-light traverse. Consequently, the impact of erroneous or embarrassing information being published can be much greater and harder to undo.

Archiving

We have always assumed that information, once published, is public—forever outside any claims to privacy. Of course, the difficulty of getting access to and then searching through old newspapers effectively returned some degree of privacy for all but the most public of figures. But the electronic elephant never forgets, and the electronic retriever is ruthless in sniffing out relevant information. Modern communications technology gives everyone potential access to this new menagerie.

Example: Criminal Justice Records

Let me give just one example of how technology raises some of the tensions I have been talking about.

For many years, policy analysts have grappled with problems raised by automated criminal justice record systems, trying to balance the doubtless contributions information technology can make to law enforcement with possible threats to privacy and due process that could result from their misuse. They have framed this discussion in terms of such issues as—what should be in the files? How accurate should they be and how should accuracy be guaranteed? How complete must they be? Who should have access to them? And, how should they be used—what types of law enforcement actions can and should be based on them?

Based on many years of debate, federal, state, and local authorities have established rules controlling access and use by law enforcement and mandating certain standards of data quality and completeness.

Reporters, on the other hand, tend to think they should have access to those records. A recent pamphlet has been published by the *Reporter's Committee for the Freedom of the Press* titled "Police Records: A Guide to Effective Access in 50 States and D.C."

If this doesn't illustrate the tough conflict between very powerful social values, I don't know what does. On the one hand, despite the efforts of authorities, these systems do contain a great deal of inaccurate and incomplete information. (On occasion, when the information is erroneous, law enforcement officials insist on keeping it in the file.) Furthermore, these systems may contain more than just official records such as arrests, indictments, convictions or acquittals, and so on. They often also hold information used for tracking people or they can contain investigative information, including associations, rumors, the gossip of neighbors, and anonymous tips.

Because of the nature of the information held in these files, an elaborate set of rules and restrictions concerning what may be put in the system and how it may be used governs the actions of criminal justice authorities. (We should note, however, that many civil liberties advocates think the rules are not nearly strong enough or enforced adequately.)

On the other hand, the need to monitor the behavior of the criminal justice system is deeply imbedded in our system of government. In order to prevent the "star chambers" and other abuses that are rampant in some countries, public scrutiny of the proceedings is not only mandatory, but a vital protective mechanism for our liberties. For that and similar reasons, the press's demands for access need to be considered. However, in accessing these files, the press is not under the same restrictions and caveats that cover law enforcement officials. Reporters may not understand or, worse, may not care about, the limitations of the data in the files. Furthermore, according to the *Reporter's Committee*, in many states, using official records as a data source is a strong defense against suit for libel.

Future systems may well be expended, as some would like to see, to incorporate more investigative data and even to incorporate statistical or artificial intelligence software. This software would "interpret" incomplete data and determine that an individual "might be" a wanted criminal or "predict" the likelihood that a person may have committed a crime.

It's a tough problem, and getting tougher.

New Questions

I will finish with three policy questions that I think are raised by new technology and that will need to be addressed, not just by journalists, but by all of us. They are not the only questions that could be addressed—perhaps you can think of others. Nor is the form in which I present them necessarily that in which they will arise—perhaps you can improve them. But they seem to exemplify the kinds of questions society will be asking in the next decade or two.

Does "Published" Necessarily Mean Forever Public?

It has been common to assume that information about us falls into one of two categories, public or private, and the flow between the two categories is one way only. That which is private, once made public, is public forever. Can we define some middle category of information that, although once public, access or duration of storage is limited? Is there some middle ground between published and not published (the line traditionally drawn) that takes into account how widely information was distributed and how available it was?

How Can We Assure that Corrections Are Made?

Given that a record is public, can be distributed more widely than ever before, may contain more sensitive information than previously possible, and is never lost, how can we be assured that error is corrected? Even assuming that the original source could be corrected, how could one track down all the secondary, tertiary, and so on, databases that may have the erroneous entry?

How should corrections be handled in press archives? Traditionally, printing corrections in later editions has been considered sufficient. While one would violate every principal of archiving to go back and change an original entry (as you will recall, that was Winston Smith's job), should the erroneous entries be tagged to indicate later corrections were made?

Should greater pressure be placed on the data publisher to get it right the first time through the application of liability or even strict liability law (where negligence or intent to do harm by the publisher is irrelevant to the liability)? Some observers see the law moving along those lines for electronic databases. Should and will the press be treated differently?

Who Gets Access to Data and Technology?

Should the press have fewer controls on its use of surveillance technology or access to personal databases than others, for instance, law enforcement authorities? Controls on government use of surveillance technology are based on the Fourth Amendment. Presumably, other civil and criminal laws control use by firms intent on corporate espionage or snoopy people curious about their neighbor's doings. The Privacy Act limits the ability of agencies to share and match the contents of databases with personal information, and Congress is considering strengthening the law in that area. Federal law, in the name of national security, currently controls access to photos taken by surveillance satellites.

In all these areas, the press is asserting their right to unrestricted use of powerful new surveillance technologies. If that right is sustained, what will be the consequences of (1) inconsistency, continued restrictions on others, or (2) uniformity, no restrictions on anyone? I think it is an interesting question without an obvious answer.

Conclusion

I raise these issues and questions not to chide, not to prescribe solutions, but to predict the directions I see public debate moving over the next decade or two.

I also see technology coming along with extraordinary capacity for intrusion. A very powerful institution, the press, claims a nearly unlimited right under the First Amendment to use it, saying to the rest of society, "Trust us. Would we hurt you?"

Some will inevitably answer, "I'm glad you asked. As a matter of fact, I don't trust you." And, some of the solutions that they will propose could do great harm to a free press and, as a result, to our democracy.

I hope my comments will serve to encourage you to start thinking about it.

7

Remarks

James H. Quello and Al Swift

JAMES H. QUELLO

The FCC and the telecommunications explosion has been a big learning experience for me, because frankly, I don't have any particular claim to infallibility or omniscience. No one is certain how we will implement all this advanced technology. I'm looking for answers, and I have a lot more questions than I have answers. Today, a couple of things. Henry Geller, are you in the room? I want to tell Henry that lately we've agreed on about every FCC issue except the Fairness Doctrine, so I was going to hang this on Henry, saying, "Well, Henry, how about that scarcity in the *Red Lion* case years ago? Does that scarcity still apply to proliferation that we have today?" I don't think so.

The other statement I made, repeated ad nauseam, is that if broadcasting had existed back in 1776, it would have been a primary beneficiary of our constitutional guarantees of freedom of the press and freedom of speech, because the constitutional guarantees weren't made for the benefit of media. They were made for the benefit of the people, of the public, so that you could have news and an informed electorate free of government influence or free of government control. Now in the United States, you do have news free of government control, but not completely free of government influence as long as you have a government-imposed Fairness Doctrine. I think fairness is naturally a great quality. All journalists should have it.

They should search for the truth, but I don't think it has to be mandated by government. So this is the first disagreement Henry and I have had for a long time. If he's here I wanted to give him this shot.

The other telecommunication expert is Dan Brenner. Henry Geller and Dan Brenner have two things in common, and that is, people recognize that with these bright gentlemen you can go to them and say, this is a very controversial issue. Give them either side of it and they'll develop one tremendous argument. That's the lawyer in them and they're very good. But with Dan, of course, we had a very trying issue for me.

I've been criticized for the FCC obscenity action and I don't know what to do about it, but it happened here in California. Some very rough language was used, very obscene, and the FCC agonized on what to do about it; but we had 20,000 complaints of obscenity on the air. The language on one radio program was probably unacceptable anywhere. What made it a little bit tough was that they had complied with our then existing limited ground rules acknowledging that a lot of kids have radios. You can't broadcast questionable indecency before 10:00 P.M. So I think the FCC is moving the time up to 12:00, but the offensive language, I can't repeat here without being guilty of obscenity. The only thing I can say is that we weren't plowing any new ground with our actions. We were merely enforcing an existing statute against obscenity on the air, and if you're a First Amendment man, you hesitate to do this. You think I'm really intruding on free speech, but should speech be that free? Or maybe I'm getting a little old. I grew up under different moral conditions than younger people did. I was born apparently thirty or forty years too soon. You see, I'm at the age now where I like to see X-rated and R-rated movies played backward because I like to see people get dressed and go home. So I just want to let you know, it gives me a lot of pause, I didn't know what to do about it. Nobody could possibly accept the language that we acted on, and I know that, frankly, the whole commission had problems with this issue. It wasn't just automatic. I didn't volunteer for any of it, but I was in the army for five years and two months and overseas for thirty-three months. So as far as that sexually oriented overused four-letter word is concerned, I've heard it and I've used it and I've done it. I just think there are some places where it's improper, and if it's used in combination with obscene words it could even be repulsive. So, as I said, this was a tough case for me, and all I will do in the future is take each case at a time, give it the best shot I can, and hope I don't have to come to the same conclusion.

But you know, getting back to the principal subject here, a lot of problems, a lot of questions. For example, how do we reconcile First Amendment rights, full First Amendment rights, with the statute requirement that regulates mass media in the public interest? Is this to free broadcasters from all program content regulation? If so, what claim will broadcasters have for priority allocation of spectrum over land mobile, or for mandatory cable carriers to reach the areas they're licensed to serve if there's no public interest claim? Also, if this is the case, and there's no longer a requirement to serve the public interest, should broadcasters be assessed a significant fee for use of a valuable national spectrum? These are troublesome questions that arise. If cable service to a community is viewed as a First Amendment right as in the initial *Preferred* case, without need for a franchise, then why should cable have to pay a franchise fee? Why not a more reasonable, say, right-of-way fee? I think application of the full First Amendment print model to the electronic media impacts much more than program content. It also will affect rules that are designed to regulate the competitive relation of the media in a balanced marketplace, and then you will have other problems. What about access? What about obscenity? What about cross-ownership? What about must carry? Questions, no easy answers.

Another question is how are local, community-oriented television stations to survive the future coming of DBS? The very foundation of the current broadcast system is localism. That's based upon Section 307(b) of the Communications Act of 1934. Eventually, maybe more homes will have home satellite receivers, and it could make sense for the networks at that time to feed their networking program directly into the home, have their advertising go directly into the home. They can bypass the affiliates. And satellite is a great nationwide distribution system, great even for international communication—for all kinds of potential for international building of understanding and good will. It is not primarily local medium. What happens with programs coming from satellites directly into the home to the ability of local stations to provide a viable local news and public affairs program? That's certainly a problem.

We have one further all-important development, and that is we are seeing more and more fiber optics installed. With fiber optics, of course, comes a tremendous varied capacity available to each household—cable, broadcasting, newspapers, computer services. That's where your electronic journalism will be most effective. Fiber optics can do everything—data processing right from your home. You could access databases through fiber optics. So what about this? How do you reconcile the monopoly power of fiber optic phone companies with competition in an open, even marketplace? Cable broadcasting does not have that assured income from the phone monopoly to cross-subsidize a system. Can we do it through a separate subsidiary? If so, how separate? What is separate? So the potential of First Amendment application to advanced communications is mind-boggling. Unfortunately, so are the solutions to the problems, and I'm here to learn. I've learned a lot. I will listen attentively and thanks for having me.

AL SWIFT

You want to know about the future of the First Amendment from a congressional policy perspective; the kinds of things that we here in Congress will be dealing with. In thinking about that topic, I was reminded of somebody who once said that when a reporter or an editor comes to you with concern about the First Amendment, it's probably sincere. When a publisher comes to you with a concern about the First Amendment, he's probably worried about his mail subsidy. Or in more recent years, whether he can be carrying tobacco advertising. The distinction, which is obviously unfair as are all over-simplifications, is important nevertheless in one respect. I think that as technology drives us into the future, the First Amendment will be used by some as a convenient hook on which to hang issues that are something less than central of the First Amendment questions in order to simply find a high moral ground from which to conduct the battle for economic turf. Public policy makers are going to have to be alert for that.

On the other hand, I think that it will be very easy to miss some legitimate First Amendment issues simply because they will be popping up in unfamiliar contexts. I'll give you a couple of examples of both of these.

You all remember how in 1980 all three broadcast networks predicted that Ronald Reagan had won the election before the polls were closed in many states all across the country. The practice continued in 1984 in New York where television stations in New York City predicted that Mondale had won the primary over Gary Hart about two and a half hours before the polls had closed in New York. We had many hearings on that and we wrestled back and forth and screamed and shouted. The First Amendment was raised constantly by the industry. And yet, I am morally certain that nobody at any network ever sat down and said let's take exit polls so that we will be able to predict elections before the polls are closed. Rather the technology to do it, in this case it was polling technology, suddenly developed. Someone said, let's take exit polls so that we will learn something about the demographics of the electorate, who voted for whom and why. All of that was useful information, and then one day, somebody who was probably decidedly not at a high policy level, and with the First Amendment the farthest thing from his mind, competition being the first thing in his mind, said, "Hey, why don't we use this to help us project who's going to win?" I honestly do not believe that in any of the networks anybody ever sat down and thought through the policy implications of predicting elections with that kind of statistical data prior to polls being closed. Once it started to happen, the industry was in a position of having to defend itself, and what better defense than to wrap themselves in the First Amendment, perhaps legitimately so, perhaps not. The fact is that we were able to work out agreements with all three networks that do not violate the First Amendment but do acknowledge that there were some very serious questions about the journalistic propriety of that particular practice.

Let me give you another example. Newspaper publishers are very concerned these days lest the telephone industry be permitted to get into the information delivery. Now on the surface that just sounds like a turf battle, and clearly there are elements of turf battle about it. But what the newspapers express, both privately and publicly, is a concern that shouldn't be totally dismissed, and that is that they are in the news business. If the telephone business, which has a common carrier mentality, is able to siphon off the profits from those who are in the business of news, what are the public policy implications? Where do you get that basic kind of news? Would a telephone industry, if it were to get in that kind of field, only be interested in cream skimming—doing the highest profit, easiest news but neglecting the more expansive in-depth reporting? That could put the local newspaper in jeopardy as an institution in the United States.

Two questions. Is that a false kind of worry? And secondly, if it is not a false kind of worry, what other public policy options should Congress or others take in order to try to preserve local newspapers? Should we take any, or just let the marketplace do whatever it will? Or should we just say, as my senior senator used to, that "all anybody ever wanted was a fair advantage" and decide that all the newspapers are doing here is trying to preserve an advantage via getting Congress to legally preclude the telephone industry from getting into certain kinds of information services?

In summary, it seems to me that as we progress in the next years, technology is going to lengthen the arm of all kinds of people who have legitimate First Amendment protection. But, there is going to be an enormous temptation to try to wrap any economic desire these interests may have in the First Amendment in order to give it a moral superiority. Further, I would suggest that you can use that rationale with public policymakers just so often before you have cheapened the argument. Once you dull the sensitivities of a public policymaker to the First Amendment concerns, once you've called wolf so many times, you will find Congress may become less sensitive to the argument, and at some point there's going to be a legitimate First Amendment argument to be made, and the public policymaker will say, "I know, I know. I've heard that before," and dismiss it too readily. I do not mean no one should use the First Amendment. Rather I think it should be used in a way that does not cheapen it to the point that public policymakers do not take it seriously. It is going to crop up legitimately, I would suggest, in ways that will seem unfamiliar. We will need to be thoughtful if we are to continue to protect it. But if we have become desensitized to its importance, we can miss those points. So it's going to take restraint, it seems to me, on the part of those who would use a First Amendment argument as a basic defense as we move into the turf battles of the future. And it is going to take some wisdom on the part of the public policymakers to know when they have a legitimate First Amendment issue before them and when they don't. In short, on the one it requires restraint, on the other it requires wisdom. Those, however, are two of the things in shortest supply.

Chronology of First Amendment Issues

GERMANY

1456   Gutenberg prints a Bible in Mainz, Germany, using movable type. Local officials, fearing the spread of dissent and heresy, impose restrictions.

1458   Charles VII of France sends Nicholas Jensen to Mainz to find out what the new press can do.

1485   Archbishop Bertold von Henneberg asks town council of Frankfurt to censor all "dangerous publications."

1486   Frankfurt and Mainz establish secular censorship boards to supplement the church board.

1579   Frankfurt book market, one of the largest in Europe, is put under Imperial Censorship Commission, which complements the ecclesiastical commission run by the Jesuits. They regularly contribute to Cardinal Caraffa's Catholic Index, which was created in 1559.

1750   The book fair at Frankfurt fails. The catalogue lists only 42 German, 23 Latin, and 7 French titles, while 1,350 titles are published in the Germanic provinces alone.

1819	Metternich proposes centralization of the book trade under government control to "prevent the unlimited power of the book sellers who direct German public opinion." Karlsbad, Bohemia, begins policy of "preventive censorship" of political pamphlets.
1933	Goebbels uses fairness doctrine for printed press to solidify media into monolith supporting the Third Reich.

ENGLAND

1476	The new printing press arrives in England in the reign of Edward IV.
1485	Henry VII imposes prior restraint in order to prevent "forged tydings and tales."
1538	Henry VIII extends censorship to all published works.
1585	The Stationer's Company is granted a monopoly on publishing by royal decree.
1630	Only 23 master printers and 55 presses are certified in the Kingdom.
1642	"Act preventing abuses in printing seditious, unreasonable, and unlicensed pamphlets and for regulating printing and presses."
1644	John Milton publishes the *Areopagitica* three years after the demise of the Star Chamber and in reaction to act of 1642.
1911	Parliament passes Official Secrets Act. It is in force today.

THE UNITED STATES

1539	First printing press is shipped to New World by Juan Cramberger of Seville.
1733	John Peter Zenger is charged with libel in the publication of His New York *Weekly Journal*. Alexander Hamilton, Zenger's lawyer, argues that truth is a defense against libel charges. Zenger is acquitted.
1765	Patrick Henry's Stamp Act Speech is distributed throughout the colonies by underground press.
1770	News of the Boston Massacre is spread through the colonies by underground press.
1776	The Declaration of Independence is widely reported in newspapers throughout the colonies.

1787	The newly proposed Constitution is published in most American newspapers. *Federalist Papers* and responders carry on lively debate over ratification through 1788.
1789	Congress convenes and receives over 200 proposals for amendments to the new Constitution by May. A House committee led by Madison and a senate committee led by Hamilton begin consolidating the amendments. At each juncture, the language concerning freedom of expression is strengthened and amendments that would restrict freedom of expression to prior restraint or political speech are defeated. The congress submits 13 amendments to the states for ratification in September.
1791	The first two amendments are defeated. Ten are ratified on December 15.
1798	The Alien and Sedition acts are passed as France threatens the United States with war. Madison and Jefferson write the Virginia and Kentucky Resolves in protest.
1801	The Alien and Sedition Acts lapse upon Jefferson's accession to the presidency in March.
1830	President Jackson forbids the distribution of abolitionist tracts in the South.
1862	President Lincoln suspends Habeas Corpus and jails "copperhead" editors opposing his war policy.
1917	*Trading with the Enemy Act* authorizes censorship of all communications moving in or out of the U.S. and provides that translations of newspaper or magazine articles published in foreign languages can be demanded by the Post Office.
1918	Borrowing language from the Alien and Sedition Acts, the Sedition Act amends and broadens the Espionage Act of 1917 by making it a crime to obstruct the recruiting service or to write or publish disloyal or profane language that is intended to cause contempt of, or scorn for, the federal government, the Constitution, the flag, or the uniform of the armed forces.
1919	U.S. Attorney General A. Mitchell Palmer begins raids and mass arrests of Americans for sedition. In *Schenk* v. *U.S.*, Supreme Court Justice Oliver Wendell Holmes advances what becomes known as the "clear and present danger" doctrine to determine how far free expression can go. He modifies his position in *Abrams* v. *U.S.*, writing that the best of truth is by "free trade in ideas" and the "power of the thought to get itself accepted in the competition of the marketplace."

1925	In *Gitlow* v. *New York*, the court states that it is proper to apply the protections of the First Amendment to the states under the Fourteenth Amendment.
1927	In order to prevent frequency overlap, the Congress, at the behest of Secretary of Commerce Hoover, passes the Federal Radio Act. It creates the FRC and requires broadcast licensees to operate "in the public interest."
1929	The FRC denies the Chicago Federation of Labor's petition to expand programming, arguing that their programming was not in the public interest.
1931	The FRC denies a license renewal on the basis of content. In *Near* v. *Minnesota*, the court states the bedrock doctrine of freedom of press, under American law prior restraint is permitted only in very unusual circumstances.
1934	The Federal Radio Act is rewritten as the Communications Act. The FCC is created; equal access and equal opportunities provisions are strengthened.
1937	In *Associated Press* v. *NLRB*, the Supreme Court rules that "the publisher of a newspaper has no special immunity from the application of general laws."
1940	Congress adopts the Smith Act, which penalizes sedition.
1941	The FCC hands down its *Mayflower* decision in which a licensee was granted renewal contingent upon its agreement not to editorialize. "The broadcaster cannot be an advocate."
1942	In *Valentine* v. *Chrestensen*, the Supreme Court ruled that commercial speech need not be accorded the same protection as political speech if it was "purely commercial advertising" (see 1976 below).
1943	In *National Broadcasting Co.* v. *U.S.*, the Court ruled that content rules over broadcasters were constitutional.
1949	In order to correct the *Mayflower* decision and provide guidelines for serving the public interest, the FCC promulgates the Fairness Doctrine. It requires broadcasters to cover important controversial issues and to provide an opportunity for contrasting views on those issues.
1950	Congress passes the Subversive Activities Control Act, which called for the utilization of various loyalty tests for government employees. Senator Joseph McCarthy alleges that the State Department is riddled with Communist subversives.
1951	Hollywood begins "blacklisting" writers and performers, and campuses dismiss professors who either take the Fifth

Amendment or can be shown to have been members of the Communist party. The McCarthyist movement peaks with the Army-McCarthy Hearings, April to June 1954.

1959   Senator Proxmire attempts to codify the Fairness Doctrine. He is believed successful by most experts until 1986 (see below).

1963   The FCC establishes the *Cullman* Doctrine, which holds that a station broadcasting a sponsored advertisement or program on one side of a controversial issue thereafter may not refuse to present the opposing viewpoint merely because the station could not obtain paid sponsorship for the opposition presentation.

1964   In *New York Times* v. *Sullivan*, the Supreme Court rules that a public official may win a libel lawsuit only by proving that the story was false and that it was published with "actual malice."

1969   In *Red Lion Broadcasting* v. *the FCC*, the court rules that the Fairness Doctrine and its personal attack rule are constitutional basically because the electromagnetic spectrum is a scarce resource.

1971   The U.S. government attempts to prevent the publication of the Pentagon Papers by the *New York Times* by invoking national security. The Supreme Court vacated its stay and earlier court orders 15 days later.

1972   In *Branzburg* v. *Hayes*, the court rules that the First Amendment does not shield reporters from an obligation to reveal their sources when demanded for use in a criminal case.

1973   In *CBS* v. *Democratic National Committee*, the court ruled that broadcasters may refuse to sell television advertising time for discussion of controversial political issues.

1974   In *Gertz* v. *Welch, Inc.*, the Supreme Court narrows the *Sullivan* decision so that it provides full protection only for stories dealing with public officials. In *Miami Herald* v. *Tornillo*, the court rules unanimously that equal space and mandatory response laws are a clear violation of the First Amendment when applied to the print media.

1975   In *Bigelow* v. *Virginia*, the court overturned the conviction of a Virginia newspaper editor who was found guilty of running advertisements for a New York abortion referral service.

1976   In *Virginia State Board of Pharmacy* v. *Virginia Citizens Consumer Council*, the court extended First Amendment protection to commercial speech.

1978	In *FCC v. Pacifica Foundation*, the court upheld a law requiring that no broadcast speech be "obscene, indecent, or profane." Known also as the "seven dirty words" case.
1979	The U.S. government obtains a restraining order, stopping *Progressive* magazine from publishing an article on how to build a hydrogen bomb. The magazine says it obtained its material from public sources and appeals to the courts. The government withdraws its case when another magazine publishes nearly identical information to *Progressive*'s.
1980	In *Richmond Newspapers v. Virginia*, the court rules that the First Amendment gives a right to gather news about government unless said government can provide an "overriding reason" to bar the press.
1981	In *CBS v. FCC*, the court ruled that the FCC may require broadcasters to sell air time to presidential and congressional candidates.
1984	In *The League of Women Voters of California v. FCC*, the court in two footnotes questions the scarcity rationale for the Fairness Doctrine and whether it is meeting its policy goal or chilling speech. The Senate Commerce Commission conducts three days of hearings from 56 witnesses and concludes that scarcity no longer exists and that the doctrine does have a chilling effect.
1985	The FCC concludes an inquiry into the Fairness Doctrine by arguing that the doctrine is constitutionally suspect and unjustified by the scarcity rationale. The U.S. Court of Appeals strikes down the "must carry" rules as a violation of cable owners' First Amendment rights. The Supreme Court refused to review the case, so the lower ruling in *Quincy* stood.
1986	The U.S. Court of Appeals in *Telecommunication Research and Action Center v. FCC* ruled that the Fairness Doctrine was not codified and that the FCC has primary jurisdiction over its imposition. The Supreme Court did not grant cert. In *Preferred Communication v. Los Angeles,* the Court ruled that if access was available, cities could not prevent competition between cable companies in the same cities. The case was remanded for discovery.
1987	The FCC repeals the Fairness Doctrine in the *Meredith* case, whch is now under appeal. Senator Hollings and Congressman Dingell lead attempts to codify the Doctrine.

Index

Abrams v. U.S., 109
Act Preventing Abuses in Printing, Seditious, Unreasonable, and Unreliable Pamphlets and for Regulating Printing and the Presses, 11
advertising, 28, 44
Aereopagitica (Milton), 11, 108
Alien and Sedition acts, 14, 109
ANPA, 41, 42
Army-McCarthy Hearings, 111
Associated Press v. *NLRB*, 110

Bell Atlantic, 42
Bigelow v. *Virginia*, 111
Bill of Rights, 4, 5–6, 12, 33–34, 109; adoption, 13–14
BOC, 19, 41, 42
Boston Massacre, 12, 108
Branzburg v. *Hayes*, 111
broadcasting industry, 15–17, 29–30, 38–39; economics, 40–41

Cable Act (1984), 18, 27, 54, 85
cable industry, 40, 41, 44, 53, 60, 88; franchising, 22–23, 29; HBO, 36, 37; operation, 61–62; regulation, 17–18, 19, 25, 26, 27, 30, 38–39
Canada, 46, 64
Capital Cities ABC, 40
Catholic Index of forbidden books, 10
CBS v. *FCC*, 112
censorship, 10–11, 35, 107–8, 109
Charles VII, 10, 107
Chernobyl, 64
Community Television v. *Utah*, 39
Congress, 16, 17, 18, 27, 105
Constitution, 12–13, 109
criminal justice system, 96–97
Cruse v. *Ferre*, 38–39
Cullman Doctrine, 111

data bases, 19, 47
Declaration of Independence, 12, 108
Department of Defense, 68–70, 72, 73–74
Dow Jones News Service, 60–61

economics, 2–3, 39, 40–41
Electronic Communication Privacy Act, 93
electronic media, 15, 19, 35, 42–43; Hitler's controls, 10–11
England, 11, 20, 108
EOSAT, 64, 65
espionage, 10, 21, 47
Espionage Act, 109

Fair Credit Reporting Act, 85
Fairness Doctrine, 23, 24, 31, 35, 41, 101–2, 110; broadcasting, 15–17; repeal, 19, 50, 61, 112; violations, 48–49
FCC, 15, 17, 37, 38, 110, 112; obscenity, 52–53, 102
FCC v. Pacifica Foundation, 112
Federal Communications Act (1934), 35
Federal Radio Act, 110
films, 34–35
First Amendment Center for the New Media, 18–19, 39
Florida, 15, 34
foreign countries: entertainment industry, 46–47; First Amendment rights in, 45–46
France, 63, 107
franchises, 17–18, 22–23, 27, 29, 38
Frankfurt book fair, 10, 107
FRC, 110
Freedom of Information Act, 73
freedoms, 20; press, 13, 58–59, 70–71; self-expression, 28–29; speech, 4, 13, 21–22

Germany, 10–11, 107, 108
Ginsberg, Douglas, 56
Gitlow v. New York, 110
Goebbels, Joseph, 10–11, 108
Gutenberg, Johann, 9–10, 107

Hamilton, Andrew, 11, 14, 108, 109; Bill of Rights, 12–13
Hart, Gary, 56, 57
HBO (Home Box Office), 36–37, 38, 46
HBO v. Wilkinson, 37
Henry, Patrick, 12, 13, 108

Henry VII, 11, 108
Hitler, Adolph, 10–11, 108

illiteracy, 35
Imperial Censorship Commission, 10
information, 93; access to, 2–4, 5–6, 33–34, 60, 80; censorship, 10–11; collection, 83–84, 94, 95; dissemination, 95–96, 104–5; maintenance, 86, 94, 96; published, 97–98
information services, 19–20
International Telecommunications Union, 46

Japan, satellites, 63–64

Kingsley International Pictures v. *Board of Regents*, 22

Landsat Act (1984), 64, 65–66, 68, 71–72, 76
law enforcement, 96–97
The League of Women Voters of California v. *FCC*, 112
libel, 11–12, 58, 81–82, 108
licensing, broadcasting, 15, 16–17
Lincoln, Abraham, 14, 109

Madison, James, 6, 12, 13–14, 109
McCarthyism, 14, 110–11
media, 1, 34, 55, 60; credibility, 56–57; satellites, 67–69
Media Institute, 18
Metternich, Klemens, 10, 108
Miami Herald, 14–15
Miami Herald v. *Tornillo*, 14–15, 34, 59, 111
microelectronics, 94
Miller, Arthur, 86
Milton, John, 11, 108
Multichannel Multipoint Distribution Service, 37
Multipoint Distribution Service, 36
Murdock, Rupert, 40
must-carry rules, 52

NAB, 17
NASA, 63

INDEX

National Broadcasting Co. v. *U.S.*, 110
Near v. *Minnesota*, 36, 110
New England, 11–12
New Hampshire, 13
news, 44; electronic media, 60–61; popular stories, 57–58; remote sensing, 64–66
newspapers, 24, 25, 26, 40–41, 42, 59, 104, 109; colonial, 11–12; German fairness doctrines, 10–11
New York, 13
New York Times v. *Sullivan*, 22, 111
New York Weekly Journal, libel suit, 11–12
NOAA: Landsat Act, 65–66; regulations, 71–72

obscenity, regulating, 37, 52–53, 102
Official Secrets Act (England), 108
OPSEC (Operation Security), 71

Pacifica Broadcasting, 38
Pacific Telesis, 42
Pennsylvania Frame, 12
Pennsylvania Ratification Convention, 13
politics, 10–11, 35, 44, 45, 104
pornography, regulating, 37–38
Preferred Communication v. *Los Angeles*, 112
printing guilds, 10
printing presses, 9–10, 11–12, 107, 108
privacy, 79, 82–83, 93, 94; invasion, 80–81; public figures, 85, 87–88, 89, 91; violations, 84–85
Privacy Act, 86, 98
propaganda, Third Reich, 10–11
public broadcasting, as public trustee, 50–52
public figures, privacy, 85, 87–88, 89, 91–92
public interest, defining, 49–50

radio, 35
Radio Act (1927), 35
Reagan administration, 3, 47
Red Lion Broadcasting v. *the FCC*, 34, 111

remote-sensing: media market, 64–66; national security, 66–69, 75; satellites, 63–64
Richmond Newspapers v. *Virginia*, 112
Roosevelt, Franklin D., 14

Satellite Master Antenna Television, 37
satellites, 37, 76; information flow, 44, 45–46, 74; media, 67–68; national security, 66–68, 69–70; remote-sensing, 63–64
Schenk v. *U.S.*, 109
security, 4, 70–71, 73–74, 75; satellites, 66–69
Sedition Act, 109
Soviet Union, 3, 45–46, 64, 74
Spot 1, 63
Stamp Act speech, 12, 108
STAR sensor, 65
State Secrets Act (England), 20
Stationers Company, 11
Subversive Activities Control Act, 110
Supreme Court, 21–22, 24, 38, 39, 59, 111; Fairness Doctrine, 16–17; films, 34–35

Telecommunication Research and Action Center v. *FCC*, 112
telephone companies, 19–20, 41, 42
television, 35, 44–45, 81
Third Reich, 10–11, 108
Trading with the Enemy Act, 109

U.S. West, 42
Utah, cable regulation, 37–38, 39

Valentine v. *Chrestensen*, 110
video distribution, 43
Video Privacy Action (1987), 83
Virginia Ratification Convention, 13
Virginia State Board of Pharmacy v. *Virginia Citizen's Consumer Council*, 111

Watergate, 84–85

Zenger, John Peter, libel suit, 11–12, 108

About the Editors and Contributors

TONY ACONE is president of Prime Ticket Network, a company engaged in sales of tickets to sports events through electronic transactions and is an executive of the California Cable Television Association.

DANIEL L. BRENNER is director of the Communications Law Program at the University of California in Los Angeles. Prior to assuming his present position in 1986 he was senior advisor to FCC chairman Mark Fowler. Earlier in his career at the FCC he had been legal advisor to both Fowler and Fowler's predecessor, Charles Ferriss. Brenner earned his B.A., M.A., and J.D. degrees from Stanford.

LEE BURDICK is acting director of the First Amendment Center for the New Media, a program of the Media Institute in Washington, D.C. She is an attorney and formerly served in the office of then FCC Commissioner Mimi Weyforth Dawson. She is the author of the paper "Electronic Databases: The First Amendment and the Militarization of Electronic Information Exchange."

HENRY GELLER is director of the Center for Public Policy Research, a Duke University think tank in Washington, D.C. He also holds a professorship at Duke. Before joining the Duke faculty he had been assistant secretary of commerce and director of the National Telecommunications and Information Administration. From 1970 to 1973 Geller was special assistant to FCC Chairman Dean Burch and in the 1960s General Counsel to the FCC.

EDWIN H. JAMES for more than 20 years was executive editor of *Broadcasting* magazine, the trade magazine of the broadcasting industry. James retired from that position in 1982 and since then has functioned as senior editorial consultant, an assignment that has kept him on the job for three full days each week. He is a graduate of the University of Southern California.

DAVID LAVENTHOL is president of the Times Mirror Company of Los Angeles, a position he has held since early 1987. He had been group vice president from 1981 to 1985 and became a senior vice president in 1986. He had previous newspaper experience at the *Saint Petersburg Times*, the *New York Herald Tribune*, the *Washington Post* and *Newsday*, where he had been successively associate editor, executive editor, vice president, and executive vice president, before moving to *Newsday*'s parent, the Times Mirror Company. Laventhol earned his bachelor's degree at Yale and his master's at the University of Minnesota.

PATRICK D. MAINES is president of the Media Institute. Prior to accepting his present position he was assistant publisher of the *National Review* and the Columbia *Journalism Review*.

ELLIOT E. MAXWELL is executive director, Strategic Planning, External Affairs, of the Pacific Telesis Group. He was previously the company's director of strategic policy analysis. He has served as deputy chief of the Office of Science and Technology for the Federal Communications Commission and special assistant to the chairman.

SIG MICKELSON is an adjunct professor in the College of Professional Studies and Fine Arts at San Diego State University and a research fellow at the Hoover Institution. He has previously served as president of CBS News, president of RFE/RL, Inc., and a vice president of Time-Life Broadcast.

ELENA MIER Y TERAN is director of special projects in the College of Professional Studies and Fine Arts at San Diego State and served as director of conference planning and organization for the "First Amendment—Third Century Conference."

J. RICHARD MUNRO is chairman and CEO of Time, Inc. His career at Time spans more than 30 years since he joined *Time* magazine's circulation staff in 1957. He has served *Sports Illustrated* as business manager, general manager, and publisher. He assumed a corporate vice presidency in 1971 with responsibility for the books, film, and cable divisions. In 1979 he was promoted to the corporate executive vice presidency and in 1980 to president and chief executive officer. He took his present post in 1986. Munro is a graduate of Colgate University and served in the Marine Corps during the Korean War.

JAMES H. QUELLO has been a member of the Federal Communications Commission since 1974. He is a graduate of Michigan State University and has served as general manager of the Goodwill Stations in Detroit and as a vice president of Capital Cities Broadcasting. From 1940 to 1945 he was in the Army of the United States where he attained the rank of major.

JOHN REDPATH, JR. is senior vice president and general counsel of Home Box Office. He is responsible for all legal aspects of HBO's operations and directs consideration of all First Amendment issues that affect the company. He joined HBO in 1978 and was appointed to his present position in 1983.

EDWARD T. REILLY, Jr., is president of the McGraw Hill Broadcasting Company. He joined the broadcasting company as executive vice president for planning and administration in 1985 and became president a year later. Most of his McGraw Hill experience has been in the McGraw Hill Book Company, where he served as executive vice president immediately before transferring to the broadcasting company. He is a graduate of Saint Francis College in New York.

J. LAURENT SCHARFF is a member of the Washington, D.C., law firm of Pierson, Ball and Dowd. He serves as counsel to the Radio and Television News Directors Association. Prior to obtaining a law degree from Harvard he was a broadcast reporter at WDSU-TV in New Orleans and WGN-TV in Chicago. He has an undergraduate degree from Northwestern University.

RICHARD M. SCHMIDT, Jr., is a partner in the Cohn and Marks law firm in Washington, D.C. He serves as general counsel to the American Society of Newspaper Editors. Schmidt was general counsel for the United States Information Administration. He is a graduate of Denver University and also obtained his law degree there.

CRAIG R. SMITH is president of the Freedom of Expression Foundation in Washington, D.C., a position he has held since 1983. He has served as a consultant to CBS News for political conventions and election night coverage and has been a speech writer for President Gerald Ford and Lee

Iaccoca. He has a Ph.D. degree from and has served on the faculty at San Diego State University.

AL SWIFT is a member of Congress from the state of Washington. He was first elected to serve in the 86th Congress and has been returned to office in each election since. Congressman Swift is a member of the subcommittee on telecommunications and finance of the House of Representatives. Before entering Congress he had been public affairs director of Station KVOS-TV of Bellingham, Washington, and administrative assistant to Congressman Lloyd Meeds.

JACK E. THOMAS is a major general (ret.) in the United States Air Force. He is currently serving as a consultant to the assistant secretary of defense in the area of Command, Control, Communication, and Intelligence (CCCI). General Thomas has spent 45 years in intelligence assignments for the USAF, for the Director of Central Intelligence and for the office of the secretary of defense. He is a graduate of the University of Utah and at one time served as a reporter for the *Salt Lake Telegram*.

FRED W. WEINGARTEN is program manager, Communications and Information Technologies, the Office of Technological Assessment of the United States Congress, an agency of the Congress responsible for long-term analysis of trends and their impact on public policy.